Samuel Johnson
1709–84

no. 83 (*see* page 117)

SAMUEL JOHNSON
1709-84

'. . . a scheme of life . . . a plan of study . . .'

KAI KIN YUNG

with essays by

JOHN WAIN, W. W. ROBSON, DAVID FLEEMAN

THE HERBERT PRESS

Copyright © 1984 The Arts Council of Great Britain and
The Herbert Press Ltd

Introduction and catalogue © 1984 Kai Kin Yung
'Reason, Bias and Faith in the mind of Johnson' © 1984 John Wain
'Johnson as a Poet' © 1984 W. W. Robson
'Dr Johnson's *Dictionary*, 1755' © 1984 David Fleeman

First published in Great Britain 1984 by The Herbert Press Ltd,
46 Northchurch Road, London N1 4EJ

Designed by Pauline Harrison
Printed in Great Britain by Jolly & Barber Ltd, Rugby
Bound in Great Britain by R. J. Acford, Chichester

British Library Cataloguing in Publication Data:
Samuel Johnson

    1. Johnson, Samuel, *1709–1784*——Exhibitions
    I. Yung, K. K.
    828'.609   PR3533

    ISBN 0–906969–45–X

Jacket: SAMUEL JOHNSON by Sir Joshua Reynolds, 1769 (detail) (no. 69)

CONTENTS

ACKNOWLEDGEMENTS

I would like to thank Mrs Mary Hyde who, despite her heavy commitment to this obviously very important Johnsonian year all over the world, has been unstinting in her generous concern, support, and encouragement to the exhibition on which this book is based; Mr Herbert Cahoon, Mr Herman W. Liebert, and Mr Roger Stoddard, for their hospitable guidance respectively to the treasures at the Pierpont Morgan Library, the Beinecke Rare Book and Manuscript Library, and the Houghton Library; Mrs Brenda Herbert and Mrs Erica Hunningher for making proof-reading such a pleasant interlude.

For their expert comments and advice I am greatly indebted to: Mr Malcolm Baker and Mr John Kenworthy-Browne on Nollekens and his bust of Johnson; Mr R. L. Bayne-Powell and Mr Jim Murrell on the miniature of Johnson after Opie (in no. 62); Mr Alec Cobbe on Reynolds's technique in his portrait of Johnson, 1769 (no. 69); Miss Lucy Cullen on the wax medallion of William Adams (no. 7); Mr Alan Cummings and Mr Jacob Simon on Reynolds's technique in general; Dr Isobel Grundy on Lady Mary Wortley Montagu's Manuscript Album (no. 5); Mr Robin Gibson and Dr John Hayes on the entries on Reynolds's first portrait of Johnson (nos 39–43); Mrs Marion S. Pottle on the Boswell Papers at the Beinecke Library; and Professor Marshall Waingrow on the passage in Boswell's manuscript for his *Life of Johnson* mentioned in no. 40, which is printed with the kind permission of Yale University and the McGraw-Hill Book Company.

In a variety of ways, warm thanks are also due to: Miss Kate Arnold-Forster, Mr Basil Barlow, Mr John Barr, Lady Frances Berendt, Mr Edwin Bronner, Dr D. B. Brown, Mrs Sally Brown, Mrs Naomi Cooper, the Dowager Countess of Crawford, Lord Dickinson, Dr J. A. Edwards, Mrs Judy Egerton, Miss Margaret Eliot and her colleagues at Dr Johnson's House, Gough Square, Mr John Fisher, Dr J. D. Fleeman, Miss Mireille Galinou, Dr Kenneth Garlick, Mr Peter Lendrum, Miss Glenise Matheson, Mr John Murray, Dr G. W. Nicholls, Miss Constance-Anne Parker, Mr Stephen Parks, Miss Jane Rick, Mrs A. Roberts, Mr Hugh Sackville-West, Mr Michael L. Turner, Mr I. A. Waters, and Miss Lavinia Wellicome.

KAI KIN YUNG

PREFACE

SAMUEL JOHNSON is one of the greatest of Englishmen. He is our greatest literary moralist in the way that Tolstoy is the greatest moralist of Russian literature. He is the greatest dictionary-maker in the history of the world and therefore the most important single figure in the history of the study of human language. He is the greatest conversationalist in British history, so influential that some of the most successful modern television figures practise their art in terms of his conversational methods. Without Samuel Johnson, Robin Day would not exist. He is Britain's greatest literary critic, a pragmatic critic who valued literature in terms of truth and reality.

Johnson is also the greatest real personality in English literature. For comparison one has to go across the boundary into fiction. Johnson is loved and his idiosyncrasies are remembered as is otherwise only true of Falstaff or Pickwick or perhaps Sherlock Holmes. Johnson's propensity for drinking tea is as familiar as Sherlock Holmes's violin.

Like William Shakespeare, Samuel Johnson was English of the English. He is nearer of course to Shakespeare than he is to us. He was born less than 100 years after Shakespeare died, and we are now commemorating the 200th anniversary of his death. He was also near to Shakespeare in origins. Birth in a small but ancient West Midlands town, his father a businessman and member of the local Corporation who ran into financial difficulties, a difficult marriage to an older woman, poverty in London and the achievement in London of literary fame and prosperity, the friendship of the London taverns, the company of actors, the patronage – but not the familiarity – of the great, the honoured age, the melancholy temperament, the patriotism – these are all characteristics of Samuel Johnson and William Shakespeare alike. That Shakespeare is an even greater literary figure is in no doubt, but Samuel Johnson was perhaps an even greater moralist.

WILLIAM REES-MOGG

TO MY WIFE JUDIE

to whom I would like to dedicate my part in this publication as an expression of my gratitude for sharing in all the anxieties and excitements from the beginning.

PUBLISHER'S NOTE

This book is based on the catalogue for the exhibition held at the Arts Council's premises at 105 Piccadilly in 1984. The exhibition was proposed to the Council by the Chairman, Sir William Rees-Mogg, as the Arts Council's contribution to the commemoration of the bicentenary of Samuel Johnson's death, and was selected by Kai Kin Yung.

INTRODUCTION

by KAI KIN YUNG

Yesterday the remains of the much lamented Dr Samuel Johnson were interred in Westminster Abbey. The procession consisting of a hearse and six horses, with the corpse, and ten mourning coaches and four, set out from Bolt-court, Fleet-street, a few minutes after twelve o'clock, being followed by several gentlemen's carriages, most of the company in which were in mourning. At one o'clock the corpse arrived at the Abbey, where it was met by Dr Taylor (who read the service), and several Prebends, and conducted to the Poets Corner, and laid close to the remains of David Garrick Esq:–

So BEGINS the report in the issue of 18–21 December 1784 of *The London Chronicle* which twenty-seven years previously, on 1 January 1757, Johnson had helped to introduce to the reader. The ceremony was economically simple and Charles Burney, knowing that it was largely the responsibility of his musical rival, Sir John Hawkins, Johnson's executor, pointed out that 'there was no anthem, or choir service performed – no lesson – but merely what is read over every old woman that is buried by the parish'. Johnson was therefore 'unworthily interred'. But for Johnson, who respected courtesy but despised pomp and ceremony, such an arrangement was appropriate to his character. He would not have wanted more.

The real significance is, however, the people who attended. Readers of *The London Chronicle* would have recognized that the occasion itself was nationally momentous. The names listed by the paper were the leading figures in the arts, politics, literature, and science of the time. The pallbearers were Sir Joseph Banks,

Bennet Langton, Edmund Burke, George Colman (the elder), William Windham, and Sir Charles Bunbury, and those attending the service included Johnson's three executors, Sir Joshua Reynolds, Sir John Hawkins, and William Scott (afterwards Lord Stowell); his doctors William Cumberland Cruikshank and Richard Brocklesby; and among the rest, General Paoli, Richard Farmer, Charles Burney, George Steevens, Edmond Malone, Joseph Priestley, George Strahan, Samuel Hoole, and John Nichols, as well as members of his household, Mrs Desmoulins and Francis Barber, his negro servant. With the exception of Mrs Thrale and James Boswell, nearly all his close friends were there. A legend in his lifetime, and in his death he made, as Hannah More says, 'a kind of era in literature'. Since then, he has remained a household name.

For this amazing posthumous publicity much of the credit must go to Boswell. There will always be Johnsonians who are in fact, as David Nichol Smith calls them, Boswellians, just as there will always be readers of the biographies of Milton, Wordsworth, Dickens, Ruskin, or Hardy who are content to have mere casual interest in their works. As Johnson writes, 'Those parallel circumstances and kindred images, to which we readily conform our minds, are, above all other writings, to be found in narratives of the lives of particular persons.'

Within the elegant confines of the Arts Council's Chamber Room, this commemorative exhibition aims to show something of Johnson's versatility as a thinker and writer, and his profound humanity, which have attracted followers and admirers here and abroad. The story of the bookseller's son from Lichfield, awkward looking, half blind, without a degree, who, without any support, started his career in London as a Grub Street hack and became a 'literary colossus', is still more captivating if told in its proper sequence. The exhibition therefore follows roughly a chronological pattern, and is divided in eight sections of which the first seven concern his life, and the last some biographies by his contemporaries. It focuses on two main features: (1) his method and career as a writer, and (2) the principal portraits of him from life.

In his masterly summary of Johnson's unique qualities, Boswell stresses his 'art of thinking and art of using his mind' as superior to those of other learned men of the time. Boswell was perfectly qualified to make such a statement. For, like Reynolds and other friends of Johnson, Boswell 'studied him, and knew him well', 'venerated and admired him'. Boswell was also acquainted with some of the most learned men in Europe: David Hume, James Beattie, Rousseau, and Voltaire, besides the Johnsonian galaxy. Slovenly in his personal appearance and chaotic in his domestic arrangements, Johnson was by contrast artistically meticulous when expressing his ideas in conversation and in writing. In this shrewd observation, Johnson is likewise reminding himself of the standard he must keep:

> A transition from an author's book to his conversation is too often like an entrance into a large city, after a distant prospect. Remotely, we see nothing but spires of temples, and turrets of palaces, and imagine it the residence of splendour, grandeur, and magnificence; but when we have passed the gates, we find it perplexed with narrow passages, disgraced with despicable cottages, embarrassed with obstruction and clouded with smoke.

Of Johnson's power, wisdom, and humour, in his conversations, there are innumerable examples in the contemporary accounts by his friends. Reynolds's *Jeu d'Esprit* (no. 73) demonstrates not only how talented a Johnsonian imitator he is but how forceful and convincing Johnson can be speaking for or against a subject. Sometimes, however, in his anxiety to 'talk for victory', what Johnson said in jest was taken in earnest.

But as a man and a writer, Johnson's principles were consistently sincere, honourable, and pure. In the concluding essay of *The Rambler*, he says that his intentions 'will be found exactly conformable to the precepts of Christianity, without any accommodation to the licentiousness and levity of the present age. . . . I shall never envy the honours which wit and learning obtain in any other cause, if I can be numbered among the writers who have given ardour to virtue, and confidence to truth.' And in the Preface to his *Dictionary* he admits that he has devoted his book, 'the labour of years, to the honour of my country'. The evidence of how he struggled within himself to achieve these ideals, and the documentary proofs of the peculiar qualities of his genius, some of which had been examined by Hawkins, Boswell, and Mrs Thrale, have remained untraced or undetected for over a century. Of the manuscripts shown in this exhibition, nearly all have been rediscovered in this century, including the manuscripts of his best known poems, *London* and *The Vanity of Human Wishes*, which are being shown for the first time in this country. Johnson's diaries, with the exception of the accounts of his journeys with the Thrales to Wales and to France, provide few commentaries of his daily activities or his friends. Sporadic as they are, they are in essence cross-examinations of his mind and soul. He repeatedly made resolutions to study, rise early, put his rooms or books in order, to conquer scruples (no. 62), to be devout and virtuous. Johnson the philosopher and moralist (defined as 'one who teaches the duties of life' in his

Dictionary) was therefore constantly reviewing his own mind and attempting to refine his principles. From his amusing attempt as an undergraduate in 1729 at calculating if by reading a certain number of lines in a day how many he could read in a year (no. 9) to the brief reference to 'a little Dutch' in October 1782 when he was obviously distressed at the thought of bidding farewell to his second home, Streatham Park (no. 87), Johnson's curiosity ('one of the permanent and certain characteristics of a vigorous intellect') and thirst for knowledge are evidently clear.

Moreover, Johnson the tireless investigator of life and study had an exceptionally retentive memory. 'Memory is the purveyor of reason, the power which places those images before the mind upon which the judgement is to be exercised, and which treasures up the determination that are once passed, as the rules of future action, or grounds of subsequent conclusion.' With this extraordinary power Johnson gathered the best authorities from his comprehensive reading to illustrate the meanings of words in his *Dictionary*. Most of his creative works were composed in the head, and he was able to 'form and polish large masses by continued meditation' before committing them to paper. Two illustrations of him exercising this power can be seen in the manuscript of *The Vanity of Human Wishes* (no. 23) and in the process of his writing the *Life of Alexander Pope* (nos 94–6): the former written in half lines, and the latter when, past his 70th birthday, Johnson turned his very brief sets of notes into his longest and perhaps his best piece of biographical and literary criticism. These confirm Malone's account of Johnson telling Burney 'that he never wrote any of his works that were printed, twice over'. This explains to some extent why so few manuscripts exist for so prolific a writer.

Very few writers in the eighteenth century had the opportunity or the means to engage portraitists. To be self-supporting and successful was not then (and even now) an easy matter. For Johnson when, at last, five months before his 46th birthday, he achieved national recognition by the publication of his *Dictionary*, there was hardly anything left in his pocket, having paid off his secretaries. He was certainly not in a position to have his portrait painted. Strangely, neither did his publishers think of having a frontispiece to these monumental volumes. Fortunately, his friend Joshua Reynolds recorded this literary triumph (no. 39). Even though it had undergone some mysterious changes, this first known portrait remains a forceful image of Johnson at the peak of his career – 'a studious thinking man', to use Reynolds's phrase, quill in hand, pausing for inspiration. For the remaining twenty-eight years of his life Johnson was portrayed by no less than twelve artists, including three more images by Reynolds himself. Allowing that four of these might well have got their ideas originally from one of Reynolds's, the number is still impressive, surpassed only by the portraiture of Pope whose financial and social status never presented any obstacle. The names include, besides Reynolds, James Barry, Nollekens, James Northcote, Frances Reynolds, John Opie, and Zoffany (regrettably untraced).

Johnson, for his part, was well aware of the tribute and value Reynolds's first portrait meant. Three years after it was painted, not only was he to urge Reynolds not to be completely distracted by 'historical pictures': 'I should grieve to see Reynolds transfer to heroes and to goddesses, to empty splendour and to airy fiction, that art which is now employed in diffusing friendship, in reviving tenderness, in quickening the affections of the absent, and continuing the presence of the dead', he was also to repay the compliment by asking Reynolds to become a contributor to *The Idler* (no. 57) and put for the first time his artistic ideas into print. The portraits of Johnson included in this exhibition amply demonstrate his point. Only the realism in Trotter's etching (no. 109), and the pathos in the death-mask bust (no. 105) bear traces of Johnson's features which frightened Boswell on their first encounter. The rest, despite Reynolds's modest denial of the portraitist's ability, do seem to 'go deeper and investigate the peculiar colouring of his mind': the classical scholar wrestling with an idea (no. 69), the voracious reader absorbed in his book (no. 78), the vivid (some may say aggressive) confrontation of the inquisitor (no. 92), or the benign sage (no. 99), all of which help to illuminate the 'greater' soul Mrs Thrale speaks of. Reynolds's portrait for Streatham Park (no. 83), however, of the large corporal frame with a tormented expression, is an uncomfortable reminder of the moralist seeking for truth. Unable to maintain regularity of habits, and reluctant to exert physical effort to work, Johnson more than often considered his life 'immethodical, and unsettled'. 'I proposed myself a scheme of life, and a plan of study, but neither life had been rectified nor study followed.'

REASON, BIAS AND FAITH IN THE MIND OF JOHNSON

ONE MORNING in March 1778, Samuel Johnson was at breakfast with his much younger friends Hester Thrale and James Boswell, both of whom were parents, and took the opportunity to give them a piece of advice about the upbringing of their children. The narrator is Boswell:

> . . . while we were at breakfast, Johnson gave a very earnest recommendation of what he himself practised with the utmost conscientiousness: I mean a strict attention to truth, even in the most minute particulars. 'Accustom your children (said he) constantly to this; if a thing happened at one window, and they, when relating it, say that it happened at another, do not let it pass, but instantly check them; you do not know where deviation from truth will end.' . . . Our lively hostess, whose fancy was impatient of the rein, fidgeted at this, and ventured to say, 'Nay, this is too much. If Dr Johnson should forbid me to drink tea, I would comply, as I should feel the restraint only twice a day; but little variations in narrative must happen a thousand times a day, if one is not perpetually watching.' JOHNSON: 'Well, Madam, and you *ought* to be perpetually watching. It is more from carelessness about truth than from intentional lying, that there is so much falsehood in the world.' (*Life*, III, 228)

Johnson himself was a stickler for truth, recoiling not only from intentional falsehood but, as the above indicates, from mere carelessness in matters which could not in themselves have much importance. He held the habit of veracity to be an essential ingredient of the moral life, and veracity included accuracy. However hard he was at work, he would never permit his servant Frank Barber to fend off uninvited visitors by uttering the polite formula that he was 'not at home'. If Frank once became accustomed to handing out even so trivial and conventional a falsehood, habits of untruthfulness might grow on him, in which case Johnson's own instructions might have started Frank on the downward path – a thought that was unendurable to him.

In conversation, Johnson bristled at any passing on of false information, whether it arose from mere carelessness and inattention, or whether it was done for effect, to make a good story. He had no patience with the kind of striking anecdote of which people say, '*Si non è vero, non è mal trovato*'. To him, such tales were always *mal trovato*. Objective reality, an opaque order of realities that were solidly out there, existed for him and was important as a part of God's creation. He bestowed small time on any notion that we create the world in the way we perceive it. When asked about Bishop Berkeley's theory of subjective idealism, he struck his foot against a large stone and said, 'I refute Berkeley *thus*.' Acknowledged authority on language as he was, he saw the function of language to describe and systematize, not in any sense to create, for, as he remarked in the Preface to his *Dictionary*, 'I am not yet so lost in lexicography as to forget that words are the daughters of earth, and that things are the sons of heaven.' 'Things' – the concrete realities – are not to be displaced by fancy. They have the authority that comes of being 'the sons of heaven', direct expressions of the will of the Almighty. This is the Johnson who took an interest in the physical world, who conducted experiments in chemistry, followed the achievements of his day in practical science and engineering, and questioned the Hebridean islanders about their methods of agriculture. Boswell records his disapproval of 'an acquaintance of ours, whose narratives, which abounded in curious and interesting topics, were unhappily found to be very fabulous.' (The man in question was probably George Steevens.) Boswell tried to urge a defence:

> I mentioned Lord Mansfield's having said to me, 'Suppose we believe one *half* of what he tells.' JOHNSON: 'Ay; but we don't know which half to believe. By his lying we lose not only our reverence for him, but all comfort in his conversation.' (*Life*, IV, 178)

To say of a man that there was no comfort in his conversation was a very grave condemnation when uttered by Johnson, the sociable being, happy where there was conversation and the play of ideas, the man who described 'a tavern chair' as 'the throne of human felicity', who said, 'We'll fold our legs and have our talk out.' But so it was. Though he enjoyed talk, he did not enjoy every kind of talk. He required it to be based on solid information and to proceed by rational stages. He had no relish for the merely fanciful. There have been some great talkers – Oscar

Wilde, for example, or Mark Twain, or an Irish leprechaun like James Stephens – whose talk Johnson would not have enjoyed, would scarcely have endured. He relished neither the nimble paradox nor the tall story. Boswell duly noted his opinion that 'The value of every story depends on its being true. A story is a picture either of an individual or of human nature in general; if it is false, it is a picture of nothing.' The context shows that Johnson was not attacking imaginative fiction as such, but the fanciful anecdote which the speaker usually claims either to have experienced or to have gained at first hand.

Johnson, then, was deeply committed to truth. But not exactly in the same way as the generation of rationalist doubters and scientific enquirers who came shortly after him. To them, truth was a religion in itself. To Johnson, it was ancillary to the practice of a religion. To them, truth was a crusade, the pushing back of the walls of darkness. To Johnson, truth was a habit of mind, part of the submission of man to the will of God. They saw falsehood as leading mankind into ignorance and slavery. Johnson saw it as a bad habit or an unfortunate mental disability like kleptomania.

It follows that Johnson's cultivation of truth was very much part of his general adherence to rationality. It did not, for instance, carry with it the obligation to undertake abstruse research or to unearth small facts for their own sake. In his professional work as a lexicographer and literary historian, Johnson undertook very little in the way of research. He systematized and clarified what had already been amassed. His last major work, *The Lives of the Poets*, contains an extraordinary amount of information about the life and work of poets who lived in the century, more or less, prior to its publication. But that information comes from Johnson's memory, from his long and wide acquaintance with literary life in England, from the fact that he had talked with many of the men he wrote about and witnessed many of the scenes he described. He set very little store by the kind of minute research into detail that is taken for granted by modern literary history. He considered Dryden as one of the greatest poets of the period he was dealing with, and shows a deep acquaintance with the circumstances of Dryden's life and work; but in that very *Life* he remarks that exhaustive biographical enquiry, even in the case of so important a figure, is little more than a waste of time. He is willing to hand on the knowledge that he has, and it is much; but he is not willing to undertake research, for: 'To adjust the minute events of literary history is tedious and troublesome: it requires, indeed, no great force of understanding, but often depends upon inquiries which there is no opportunity of making, or is to be fetched from books and pamphlets not always at hand.'

To Johnson, then, not all truths were equal. What he valued was the truth that tends to illuminate 'general nature', not the idiosyncratic or the anomalous. The mere fact that something was true did not necessarily make him see it as valuable. That position was reserved for the nineteenth-century enquirers. His adherence to 'general nature' meant that he felt obliged to discourage any anecdote or example that highlighted the strange, the odd, the peculiar. If anyone had managed to bring him absolutely firm proof that, say, a Norfolk villager had taught a pig to play the violin, he would not have been much interested. What interested him was the general position. (Norfolk villages are not as a rule much different from other villages; pigs do not play the violin.) By the eighteenth century the great trade routes of the world had mostly been opened up, and Johnson was acquainted with many people who had travelled widely. But he was sharply suspicious of any story of strange practices or paradoxical convictions among distant peoples. Riding with Boswell through the Hebrides, discoursing in a leisurely way out of the rich stores of his mind, he spoke of Montesquieu, whom he allowed to be 'a fellow of genius': but,

> Whenever he wants to support a strange opinion, he quotes you the practice of Japan or of some other distant country, of which he knows nothing. To support polygamy, he tells you of the island of Formosa, where there are ten women born for one man. He had but to suppose another island, where there are ten men born for one woman, and so make marriage between them.

Johnson habitually argued in this way because he took it that truth was served by the general example, the one that would hold in a majority of cases. He believed that it was the destiny of all great men and women, and of all remarkable actions, to end up enshrined in precept and maxim. Their names and deeds would be rendered down, so to speak, into the common wisdom of humanity. Thus of Flora MacDonald he writes, 'a name that will be mentioned in history, and if courage and fidelity be virtues, mentioned with honour.' And, even more pithily, of the great Swedish conqueror Charles XII,

> He left the name, at which the world grew pale,
> To point a moral, or adorn a tale.

The cast of Johnson's mind was forensic ('FORENSIC: Belonging to courts of judicature'), and the reason why talking with him was such a bracing exercise was that he carried the practice of examining evidence into everyday life. He was also lawyerly in his appetite for disputation. The law proceeds by question and cross-question in an attempt to work towards the facts. Johnson believed in this method, to the extent that he would often, in a playful spirit, take what he personally considered to be the shakier argument and press it home vigorously to stretch his opponent's mind to the uttermost. There is an obvious value in this. Defence of even an accepted truth must never grow flaccid.

This has some bearing on the hoary old subject of Johnson's 'prejudices'. The popular caricature of him as a comic bundle of predictable opinions, mostly re-actionary, is by now presented by no one with any claim to literacy. On the other hand, it is a strange and not particularly valuable kind of person who reaches middle age without some fixed principles and firm beliefs which he feels bound to state and defend. Johnson made no secret of his principles and beliefs. Anyone who knew him at all knew that he was a Tory (within the political divisions of his time, which are not necessarily those of ours), that he was a royalist, that he was a Christian, and that he believed in 'subordination', by which he meant an acceptance of ranks in society rising one above another. (He never in his life grovelled to a duke or earl, never budged from the independent stance of a free-born Englishman, yet he accepted *in theory* the notion that a duke or earl had a higher status than he had, just as the Sovereign had a higher status than theirs.)

When Johnson entered into discussion, or put pen to paper, he did so as a professed holder of these and similar views. And this too is forensic. When a barrister takes part in a court case, he is always clearly labelled from the beginning as Counsel for the Defence or for the Prosecution, and he will not change sides half-way through. He does not come in without identification, begin to speak as if he had a completely open mind, and gradually allow his hearers to discern which way his argument is tending. Similarly with Johnson. He had no objection to treading on people's toes, provided only that it was perfectly clear beforehand whose toes he intended to tread on. The roars of outrage that resulted did little more than amuse him. These roars continued well into the next generation, when Johnson was the bogey-man of English progressives. William Cobbett, a man of stature whom Johnson would not have despised as an adversary, summed up the feeling of many people in the early nineteenth century when he wrote of Johnson: 'If the writings of this time-serving, mean, dastardly old pensioner had got a firm hold of the people at large, the people would have been bereft of their souls. These writings, aided by the charm of their pompous sound, were fast making their ways, till light, reason and the French revolution confined them to the shelves . . .'

Another turn-round of opinion was due when it became clear that the Europe ushered in by 'light, reason and the French revolution' was not all peaches and cream. Johnson has been loved and hated along predictable lines.

Did Johnson's bias, his notorious *parti pris*, ever lead him into false statement? I think the answer has to be that, here and there, it did. It coloured his perception of reality so that he misrepresented that reality to himself and thence to the reader. I shall take two examples, both from *Lives of the Poets*. The first concerns Milton. Johnson, inevitably, disapproved of Milton's politics. A republican, a regicide even; and, in religion, a campaigner against the established Church. If Johnson had been content to state this disapproval and then stand away from the picture, well and good. The problem was that Milton's psychology was opaque to him. He took it for granted that anyone who objected so strongly to conventional authority must be a sullen, hangdog fellow. He could hardly conceive that Milton could have attacked royalism and episcopacy from a thought-out position, and that this position could coexist with being witty, civilized, a good talker, pleasant company. All these things Milton was, as every domestic account of him agrees. From this basis it was an easy step, and one that Johnson naturally wished to make, to portray Milton as a difficult, stubborn man who espoused rebellious policies for their own sake: 'Milton's republicanism was, I am afraid, founded in an envious hatred of greatness, and a sullen desire of independence; in petulance impatient of control, and pride disdainful of superiority. He hated monarchs in the State, and prelates in the Church; for he hated all whom he was required to obey.'

One final touch is necessary to complete the blackening of Milton's character: he has to be shown as essentially a theorist, a man whose ideas come from books and have never been tested against the rough corners of experience. 'He had read much, and knew what books could teach, but had mingled little in the world, and was deficient in the knowledge which experience must confer.' When one thinks of the experiences which Milton had that Johnson did not – the European travel at a formative age, fatherhood, the friendship with a Court musician like Lawes and with members of an aristocratic family, the Bridgwaters, the turmoil of the Civil War, the years of working for Cromwell, the crash of his hopes in 1660 – it seems an extraordinary accusation. But it is quite consistent. It is the view generally taken by the conservative of the radical – a fellow full of fancy notions, very much head in the clouds, whose ideas have no basis in everyday reality.

The next example concerns the life of Gray. Part of the fascination of the *Lives of the Poets* lies in its historical range. At the beginning of the series, in writing the lives of men like Milton and Butler, Johnson is stating his position with regard to the great pivotal conflicts of the seventeenth century. As he draws to the end, he is writing of men whose lifetime runs alongside his own, who addressed the same reading public as he did, enjoyed or suffered the same economic conditions as he did, and had, more or less, the same opportunities. It was inevitable that a certain note of personal competitiveness should sound now and then through these later *Lives*. And nowhere more so than in the 'Life of Gray'. Gray's life was considerably shorter that Johnson's; he was born nine years later and died thirteen years sooner. And he was careful to plan that relatively short life in such a way that it contained a minimum of event. It was a life of books and of the mind. His experiences – and we must never underrate their intensity and depth, for he was a real poet – were interior. Of outward-facing action, of 'experience' in the sense in which one normally uses the term, he had, and intended to have, very little. As a young man he travelled in France and Italy at the invitation of Horace Walpole; the rest of his life was spent in the British Isles, and very nearly all of it in Cambridge, where he evidently took full advantage of the licence for cultured *accidie* offered by the eighteenth-century university. His modest material comforts supplied by the college system, his attention engaged by books and manuscripts, he seems to have lived out his life as a shy, rather fussy bachelor don: a type with which Johnson found it very difficult to sympathize. Johnson was, on the whole, no great admirer of retirement. He thought a man's duty was to give of his best in the broad daylight of life rather than hide in the dappled shade of contemplation. Fervent Christian though he was, it was somewhat grudgingly that he allowed even piety as a sufficient reason for self-immolation. A recluse of Gray's type, who made no claim to religious motivation but, in Johnson's words, 'cultivated his mind and enlarged his views without any other purpose than of improving and amusing himself', aroused in him feelings very close to disapproval. He evidently felt that Gray ought not to have chosen such an easy path through life; that he ought to have come out into the arena of ordinary existence and taken a few of its hard knocks, if only to gain the depth and wisdom necessary to address his fellow-men through the art of poetry – that art whose chief purpose, as Johnson maintained, was to help people live their lives.

It was the more annoying that in the case of Gray something seemed to have gone wrong with this theory, since he was a poet and a very good one. Johnson steadily refused to see merit in most of Gray's small output, but there was no resisting the *Elegy in a Country Churchyard*, that sombre, dignified meditation on death, not the death of distinguished men of learning such as Gray had spent his life among and such as he was himself, but the death of common people, the 'rude forefathers of the hamlet'; it celebrates 'the short and simple annals of the poor'. Johnson has throughout his brief essay repeatedly suggested that Gray's fame was a matter of fashion, that it was whipped up by a coterie, that people pretended to admire his work because to admire it was a mark of intelligence. Of Gray's two celebrated odes, 'The Progress of Poetry' and 'The Bard', Johnson reports that they were so unintelligible as to have very few readers at first, until 'Some hardy champions undertook to rescue them from neglect, and in a short time many were content to be shown beauties which they could not see.' The implication here is that Gray's fame is not fame at all, but a vogue. All the more significant is the *volte-face* when Johnson, reaching the end of his essay, suddenly praises the Churchyard elegy for precisely those virtues he has been accusing Gray of lacking: it is true to ordinary life and is loved by ordinary people.

> In the character of his *Elegy* I rejoice to concur with the common reader; for by the common sense of readers uncorrupted with literary prejudices, after all the refinements of subtlety and the dogmatism of learning, must be finally decided all claim to poetical honours. The *Churchyard* abounds with images which find a mirror in every mind . . .

Of literary prejudices, then, Johnson stands finally acquitted in the case of Gray. He undervalues the bulk of Gray's poetry, but that is within the normal right of a critic, and when he comes to the one poem that the English people have really accepted as a classic, he puts himself at their head in praising it. And yet the Life of Gray, like that of Milton, does exhibit bias, and of the same kind. It offers a portrayal of the man's personality based not so much on the concrete evidence of what he was like as on Johnson's notion of what he *ought* to have been like. Take the passage describing Gray's break with Walpole. All that we know for certain is that the two young men were travelling companions for some months, after which Gray returned home and Walpole continued his tour. Doubtless they had ceased to enjoy each other's company; it seems that they had quarrelled; in later years, after Gray's death, Walpole chivalrously took the blame for their disharmony. Johnson, however, will not let it rest there:

> . . . unequal friendships are easily dissolved: at Florence they quarrelled, and parted; and Mr. Walpole is now content to have it told that it was by his fault. If we look

however without prejudice on the world, we shall find that men, whose conscious-
ness of their own merit sets them above the compliances of servility, are apt enough in
their association with superiors to watch their own dignity with troublesome and
punctilious jealousy, and in the fervour of independence to exact that attention which
they refuse to pay. Part they did, whatever was the quarrel . . .

This is surmise, and surmise that comes very close to mere slander. Because Gray
was poor and Walpole was rich, and they were both cultivated and intelligent,
theoretically equals, it was natural for the poor one to become prickly and difficult
to get on with. This kind of thing is 'apt enough' to happen, so Johnson guides the
reader to the conclusion – without saying it in so many words – that it must have
happened in this case. In fact, there are scores of ways in which two people on a
holiday might grate on each other's nerves. Of the various hypotheses that might
be offered, Johnson picks on the one least favourable to Gray, most likely to make
him seem petulant and ungrateful, and this can only be called bias.

So much, as I see it, for Johnson's mind in its rationality and its occasional proneness
to bias. What of the part played by faith? This panel of the triptych is, I believe, the
one that adds

> a sober colouring to an eye
> That hath kept watch o'er man's mortality.

Johnson's religious faith was maintained with an effort because he had an emotional
need to maintain it. That need, and that effort, make up the tragic dimension in his
life.

The question, would Johnson have had a happier life if he had not been a Christian
believer? will seem to the convinced Christian to be merely frivolous. And I admit
straight away that I personally write from the point of view of someone to whom
the Christian explanation of the universe seems a hypothesis that has as much
chance of being true as any other hypothesis, rather than something to be accepted
on the road to Damascus. A great deal of the private anguish of Johnson's life
undeniably arose from his fear of eternal damnation. Christianity, viewed from
outside, seems to be mainly composed of threats and promises, and it is a sad fact
that the threat of eternal punishment for backsliders was very much more actual to

Johnson than the promise of eternal bliss for the righteous. With his exceedingly sensitive conscience, he could never be sure that he was one of the righteous; and if it turned out that on Judgement Day the verdict was given against him, the pit of hell yawned at his feet. Hence the piteous note of supplication in the prayers he wrote for his own use, the impression one gets that he is pleading with a tyrant little inclined to make allowance for human weaknesses.

> O Lord, forgive me the time lost in idleness; pardon the sins which I have committed, and grant that I may redeem the time misspent and be reconciled to thee by true repentance, that I may live and die in peace, and be received to everlasting happiness. Take not from me, O Lord, thy Holy Spirit. But let me have support and comfort for Jesus Christ's sake . . .
>
> Almighty and most merciful Father, whose providence is over all thy works, look down with pity upon the diseases of my body, and the perturbations of my mind . . .

Johnson clung to reason as to a handrail in an unlighted passage. But to safeguard his religious faith it was necessary for him, now and then, to let go of this handrail of reason. The effort this cost, the agony it caused, are there in the records of his life.

It was, in fact, this difficult balance that made him one of the great spokesmen for the civilization of the eighteenth century. That civilization was, in many ways, as fragile and as beautiful as a soap-bubble. The scientific revolution of the seventeenth century had altered the world-view of Western man. It took a hundred years for that revolution to filter down into a technology that changed every detail of life: from transport to education, from politics to cookery. But the altered perception did not wait for the technology. The splendid, poised, ironic civilization of the eighteenth century had its being in a time-lag. Everyday life was still pre-industrial and pre-imperial; the economy of every country was agrarian. But the moving spirit of the age, in its centres of thinking and feeling, was already rationalist and sceptical.

Such a balance could not last. And, equally, Samuel Johnson's own difficult equilibrium, achieved at huge psychic expense, could not last. With one powerful hand he reached back to the Ages of Faith. With the other, he grasped the empirical spirit of the nineteenth-century sciences.

In the event, as we know, both those adversaries have given ground. Science has become less rational, more speculative, mystical even. Religion has retreated into the fastness of metaphor. There is no longer a straight antagonism between them: what once was a battleground has now become a vast grey area, in which speculation has taken over from dogma. This is nowhere better illustrated than in Johnson's own art of literature, which he saw as making clear statements and inculcating unambiguous moral precepts. Now, with the proliferation of techniques borrowed from other disciplines such as Structuralism, and preoccupations from the social sciences and linguistic philosophy, Johnson would hardly recognize the field in which he was eminent.

In his own day, though, and in his own case, the double grip had to be attempted: at least, by one of his particular temperament. Many eighteenth-century people, faced with the apparently irreconcilable split between traditional faith and the ascendant rationality, quietly abandoned faith. Johnson never did. But neither could he abandon reason, which was the breath of his lungs. He hated the thought of submerging the dignity of a rational being: what he would have thought of our modern drug-culture can only be conjectured. Consider his discussion with Boswell about wine and drunkenness:

> BOSWELL. 'I think, Sir, you once said to me, that not to drink wine was a great deduction from life.'
> JOHNSON. 'It is a diminution of pleasure, to be sure; but I do not say a diminution of happiness. There is more happiness in being rational.' (*Life*, III, 245)

That last remark gives the key. There is more happiness in being rational. But religion is not about happiness; it is about standing well with the gods, or with God. And for Johnson, that standing well consisted not of doubts but of certainties, not of questions but of answers.

Socrates, after being condemned to death for his persistent habit of questioning fundamentals, said to his judges: 'The hour of parting is come. We go our separate ways, you to live and I to die. Which is better, only the gods know.' It is impossible to imagine Johnson ending his life on such a note of debate and discussion – ending it, in fact, with a question. He needed an affirmative. His quest for that affirmative in the shifting landscape of a century of experiment and enquiry is the diagram of his life. It gives him his tragic quality, his background of conflict and unease, the impression he conveys of being at odds with his age and yet, precisely because of the range of his preoccupations and his titanic struggle to hold them in a unity, its greatest single representative.

[24]

W.W. ROBSON

JOHNSON AS A POET

JOHNSON'S POETRY appears to be little read or discussed, even by Johnsonians (I mean readers who know him through his writings as well as the records of his conversation). There are, I think, two reasons for this.

The Dryden-Addison-Pope style in poetry is still widely disliked, in spite of helpful discussions like James Sutherland's in *A Preface to Eighteenth-Century Poetry* (1948) and Rachel Trickett's in *The Honest Muse* (1967). The discrediting of this style was one of the lasting achievements of the Romantics. During the Anti-Romantic movement of the twentieth century there was a gesture at reviving it, but, as Joseph Wood Krutch has said, many of T.S. Eliot's followers professed to admire Dryden not because they really cared about him but in order to show that they did not consider themselves Romantics. Now that the Romantics are back in favour, sailing under new colours as what Harold Bloom calls the 'Visionary Company', there is even less chance that eighteenth-century poetry will ever again be generally enjoyed. In any case, few would deny that Johnson is a lesser master than Dryden or Pope. Even in his best verse there is nothing quite so dazzling as Dryden on Achitophel or Pope on Timon's Villa.

The second reason is a common feeling that Johnson both in his theory and his practice deviated from the main tradition of English poetry in the interests of a transient 'Augustanism'. In *Tradition and Experiment in English Poetry* (1979), a wide-ranging survey of its development, Philip Hobsbaum does not even mention him. The main charge against his verse is that it lacks particularity and lively metaphor. These ideas, usually in association, have been for many years very influential in the teaching of poetry in schools and colleges. There is a strong conviction that English poetry requires such qualities to be effective, though they may not be needed in Latin or French; a line of Racine, wholly 'abstract', may have as much force as a 'concrete' line of English poetry. But English, it is held, requires the particular, the specific, the boldly metaphorical. On the other hand Johnson believed in 'the grandeur of generality'. His poetry has been thought to be abstract, colourless, conventional. It is marmoreal and inscriptional, unlike his lively talk. He is thought to have regarded poetry as the application from outside of melody and pattern to thoughts that could as well (and therefore could better) have been expressed in prose.

This account of Johnson the poet is still current in textbooks. I believe it to be quite false. It has inhibited the recognition of the great poems Johnson wrote as part of the central tradition of English poetry. I think it is a complete misrepresentation of Johnson to say that he did not favour the concrete and particular, and the vividly metaphorical, in his writing. It would be obviously absurd to say this of his conversation. Any random instance will furnish a counter-example: when Johnson was asked how he felt after the failure of *Irene* he replied: 'Like the Monument.' Some critics however (like Macaulay) while granting that Johnson *spoke* vigorously, have held that he *wrote* ponderously, in polysyllabic 'Johnsonese'. But others who knew Johnson personally testified that his talk and his writings were very similar. It is unfortunate that in an influential essay the late W.K. Wimsatt insisted on the abstractness of Johnson's prose style. To take just one example: the exuberant passage in the *Preface to Shakespeare*, in which Johnson sighs over Shakespeare's quibbles, is a positive firework display of similes and images, obviously taking an amused pleasure in doing the same sort of thing as Shakespeare. Even in less colourful passages the pressure of concrete reality is always felt behind his phrases. Anyone who has read Johnson's prose at all widely will know how absurd it is to use the term 'abstract' of it, in a pejorative sense. If that term is to be used in that sense it would be more appropriate for lacklustre Victorian prose, or even more for modern cloudlands of structuralese, than for Johnson's pungent, shipshape eighteenth-century sentences. The question of his verse is more complex, but the same considerations apply to it, as the discussions by F.R. Leavis in *Revaluation* (1936) and Christopher Ricks in 'Johnson's Poetry' (*New Statesman*, 6 August 1965) have shown. As for 'the grandeur of generality', it has nothing to do with polysyllabic abstractions. Some such expression as 'human centrality' would be a better rendering of what Johnson meant.

In short discussions I have to speak categorically. I hope the passages from Johnson's poetry that I quote below will bear out my assertions. If these are overemphatic, my excuse must be that the Romantic tradition is still prevalent, and according to that tradition Johnson was not a poet at all, except in the minimal sense given in his *Dictionary*: 'Inventor: An author of fiction; a writer of poems.' I disagree with this and believe that Johnson was essentially a poet. This is proved by the brilliance of his conversation, the best in the language. It is full of proliferating imagery, bold imaginative flights, unexpected but happy analogies, all tokens of the poet, just as wit and weightiness are tokens of the wise and strange man. As for formal verse, there are many signs that Johnson as a poet was 'born', not 'made'. His best poetry came to him easily. He was a master of improvisation. Some of his impromptus were no more than light society verse, but even here he is a poet and not merely a versifier. And other examples of his quickly composed verse are serious and noble.

Further evidence of Johnson's poethood is amply available to those who know him as a critic of English poetry. His range is here far wider, his taste more catholic, than is commonly supposed. As is usual with real poets he loved to discuss technical questions. He can discourse happily for pages on elision and caesura, the use of the Alexandrine in triplets, the preferability of rhyme or blank verse for long poems, etc. But he did not believe in recipes for writing poetry. He believed in 'inspiration' and 'originality' as much as any Romantic, in 'inwardness' and 'authenticity' as much as any Modern, though the words he used for these ideas were different. His theory of poetry was anti-intellectualist. As for imagery, so much stressed by twentieth-century criticism, he regarded it as of paramount importance. He again and again objected to its subordination to the conceptual. To give just one example: in his *Lives of the Poets* he says in depreciation of Cowley that he 'gives inferences instead of images, and shews not what may be supposed to have been seen, but what thoughts the sight might have suggested.' Johnson favoured what the moderns call 'immediacy'.

Was Johnson a major poet? His contemporaries thought so, but the twentieth century has not agreed with them. Even those who take the view that I have outlined have to admit that his best poetry is small in quantity and mostly occasional. Not that these admissions are very damning. Some famous poets, far more voluminous than Johnson, have written less great poetry. And most genuine poetry has been occasional. Still, I cannot forget Arnold's reason for ranking Wordsworth so high, 'the great and ample body of powerful work' which Arnold thought remained when the inferior work was cleared away. This could not truly be said of Johnson as a poet. But why not?

[27]

Since Johnson was a personal poet, not gifted for drama or narrative, biographical considerations cannot be avoided here. Johnson was neurotic, but he hated 'whining'. We know mostly from others about his titanic struggle against mental and bodily suffering. He himself kept quiet about it. He did not record intimate experience in verse; or if he did, it was in Latin, a second language to Johnson. (We might think here of two twentieth-century Latin poets, W.R. Inge and A.E. Housman.) One of the few passages that refer directly to his own life occurs in the touching Latin poem in which he mentions his father teaching him how to swim. (Partially paralysed people are often happy in water, which supports the body.) Another Latin poem, with a Greek title, 'Gnōthi Seauton' (Know Thyself), was composed when Johnson had completed the arduous task of the 4th revision of the *Dictionary*: it is a salute, at once wry and sombre, to a great predecessor, Scaliger, and it is the most personally revealing of his poems. His lively friend Arthur Murphy turned it into a passable imitation of his English verse, but it is impossible to imagine Johnson writing such a poem in English. No one had better earned the right to say with Whitman 'I am the man. I suffered. I was there,' and with Frost 'I have been one acquainted with the night.' But Johnson could express such thoughts only as a human being, not as a poet.

I believe that the main reason why Johnson's output was so small is the problem that sincerity presented to him as a poet. Some modern critics dismiss the question of a poet's sincerity as irrelevant, or naive. Lionel Trilling smiles at the 'engagingly archaic' quality of F.R. Leavis's attempt to discriminate in Eliot's poetry between the more and less sincere. Trilling may be right, but it doesn't matter, since Johnson believed that poets should be sincere. But this involved him in a difficulty. Poetry required artifice, fiction, and Johnson defined 'fiction' in his *Dictionary* as 'The art of feigning or invention; the thing feigned or invented; a falsehood; a lye.' No other meanings are given. We remember his objection to the mingling of fiction with 'awful truths' in *Lycidas*, and his doubts about the possibility of satisfactory devotional poetry.

In attempting to be rid of the 'sincerity' problem modern criticism has made much of the dramatic quality of poetry (and not only in plays). But we do not need to look at *Irene* to realize that Johnson could rarely personate successfully. His masks in *The Rambler* are often transparent. All the characters in *Rasselas* speak alike: the dialogue is stylized. This is not a fault, for it has made the book a classic of the world. But we do not want all drama or fiction to be like *Rasselas*. Some have accused Johnson of lack of imagination, but the truth seems to be that far from being deficient in that 'licentious and vagrant faculty' he had too much of it, and it frightened him. It 'preyed upon life'. Sober, factual truth was something he had to hold on to. Johnson was not completely in sympathy with the Anti-Romantic movement of Hobbes (who assimilated imagination to madness) and Locke. (No real poet could be, wholeheartedly.) But formality of style, the iron curtain of the eighteenth-century manner, was evidently a defence he needed. We know that at the time his mother was dying he wrote *The Idler* 41, a dissertation on the death of a friend, full of dignity and philosophic calm and adult feeling, in majestic Johnsonian periods; yet at the same moment he was pouring out letters to Lucy Porter which are full of the grief and confusion of an anguished child.

In what he wrote for a public, Johnson does not display what he called 'the wounds of the mind'. But he was a direct, open, candid writer. In *Rasselas*, in 'The Vision of Theodore', in the 'Life of Boerhaave', the feeling is heartfelt. Everyone knows how formidable he was in person, the Colossus of Literature, as Boswell called him, the Great Cham, Ursa Major; yet he was amazingly ingenuous and ready to confide in even slight acquaintances. Boswell (sometimes for dramatic purposes) can appear naive, but he was psychologically devious; Johnson was not. This straightforwardness is what makes his Prayers appealing beyond anyone else's, with their shortness and simplicity and the deep seriousness of Johnson's repeated appeals for grace to amend his life. But how far did Johnson achieve this personal quality, this stamp of experience, in his poetry?

To read through Johnson's poems in J.D. Fleeman's admirable edition is to have some surprises. Johnson's youthful work includes some pieces which suggest very different directions which his talent might have taken. The earliest poem of his to be preserved is on a daffodil! His view of the poetic art may have debarred him from minute descriptions ('numbering the streaks of the tulip'), yet there is evidence that he shared Wordsworth's feeling about nature and associated it with childhood and a sense of boundless freedom in a lost paradise. But while Wordsworth expressed this in poems such as *Tintern Abbey* Johnson reserved its expression for prose.

Another unexpected aspect of the young poet is disclosed in 'Upon the Feast of St Simon and St Jude'. This is an example of what was then called 'enthusiasm', a pejorative word. Christopher Smart could have written it: it is in the stanza of his *Song to David*.

> Where Atlas was believ'd to bear
> The weight of ev'ry rolling sphere,
>   Where sev'nmouth'd Nilus roars,

> Where the Darkvisag'd Natives fry,
> And scarce can breath th'infected sky,
> But bless the Northern shoars . . .

In later years Johnson deprecated these youthful ecstasies to Boswell, but we know from Fanny Burney's *Memoirs* that even as an older man he was subject to fits of 'enthusiasm' which obliged him to wave his arms in the air. Johnson may have belonged to the Age of Reason, but he also belonged to the Age of Sensibility. He wept over the *Dies Irae*; he wept over his 'young Enthusiast' in *The Vanity of Human Wishes*.

Some of Johnson's most accomplished poems are ostensibly inspired by music (ladies playing on the spinet or harpsichord.) These have been assumed to be frigid exercises, because he was notoriously unmusical. But when not teasing he would admit that in failing to appreciate music he lacked something essential. Not six months before his death he asked Burney to teach him 'the Scale of Musick. Teach me your language.' Music had to be for him a purely notional value, and in the 'Stella' poems he uses this art, together with the art of painting, as an evocative symbol for the ideal conduct of life.

> Mark, when the diff'rent Notes agree
> In friendly Contrariety;
> How Passion's well-accorded Strife
> Gives all the Harmony of Life:
> Thy Pictures shall thy Conduct frame,
> Consistent still; tho' not the same;
> Thy Musick teach the nobler art,
> To tune the regulated heart.

Here Johnson is close to the graceful side of Swift's verse, as in 'Cadenus and Vanessa', and to poems like Marvell's 'The Fair Singer'. As a poet Johnson descended from the Metaphysicals, to whom he gave that name.

The most beautiful of Johnson's poems in honour of music is his 'Epitaph on Claudy Phillips, a Musician', which he is said to have composed while stirring his tea.

> Phillips, whose touch harmonious could remove
> The pangs of guilty pow'r, and hapless love,
> Rest here distress'd by poverty no more,

Find here that calm, thou gav'st so oft before.
Sleep, undisturb'd, within this peaceful shrine,
Till angels wake thee, with a note like thine.

Christopher Ricks draws attention to the word 'touch' here. We should think not only of its meaning as a musical term but of Queen Anne touching the child Samuel Johnson (without success) for scrofula. There is a religious-magical suggestion, so that the 'angels' at the end do not appear merely to clinch a gracious eulogy. These poems on music should be read in the light of Dryden's great poem 'Alexander's Feast', to which Johnson alludes in 'To Miss Hickman'. In 'Alexander's Feast' the tribute to music is implicitly a tribute to the power of art generally, to the power of poetry, so that the poem celebrates itself. Johnson writes in that tradition.

It was on the strength of *Irene*, *London*, and *The Vanity of Human Wishes* that Johnson's reputation as a major poet was based in his own time. Everyone agrees that *Irene* is a failure both as drama and as poetry. It lacks 'the Johnsonian aether'; its only atmosphere is that of Drury Lane. How ironical that Johnson failed to achieve formal tragedy! The writer of *The Vanity of Human Wishes* and *Rasselas* and the 'Life of Swift', perhaps uniquely in the eighteenth century, has what Unamuno called the tragic sense of life. Yet *Irene* is dead. It was slowly and painfully elaborated, unlike Johnson's successful poems; except for an occasional cry from the heart, there was no place in it for the author's tortured feelings. It is hardly worth mentioning that there are no memorable characters and the theme is not conceived and presented dramatically; worse still, it is not even a good poem. The blank verse is that of a couplet writer who has dropped the rhymes and added from time to time an extra syllable or 'feminine ending', by which he gains nothing, and loses the opportunity for writing witty epigrams or clinching his effects. *Irene* can be read with interest for its serious political and moral reflections but as a tragedy it is cold. Yet its author's state of mind was quite otherwise.

I . . . delayed my departure for a time to finish the performance by which I was to draw the first notice of mankind upon me. When it was completed I hurried to London, and considered every month that passed before its publication, as lost in a kind of neutral existence, and cut off from the golden hours of happiness and fame. (*Rambler* 163)

But the patentee of Drury Lane was more interested in pantomimes than in classic drama, and Johnson turned to writing for *The Gentleman's Magazine*. (Thanks to Garrick he did see *Irene* staged.)

London and *The Vanity of Human Wishes* are much livelier poems, but they present readers of today with some problems. They are both 'imitations' of poems by the Roman writer Juvenal – Decimus Iunius Iuuenalis (*c.* A.D. 60–*c.* 130). This mode of writing was fashionable in the seventeenth and eighteenth centuries, but came to be suspect on the ground that an English poet is lamed by having to follow in the footsteps of his Latin original. In recent times, however, the notion of updating an ancient poem by way of 'homage' has become current through Ezra Pound and his followers. Still, Roman satire does not appeal to English tastes. It seems a meandering diatribe. The great English satires owe nothing to it; in works such as *Gulliver's Travels*, *The Dunciad*, *Erewhon*, *Animal Farm*, our writers have created their own form.

But something must be said about the relation between *London* and Juvenal's third poem. That poem is hard to interpret. Juvenal's intentions remain a subject for scholarly controversy. He has been seen as like Isaiah, scourging the sins of the Roman Babylon. On the other hand H. W. Garrod (in 1912) dismissed his poetry as 'rhetoric of rancour' and excluded him from the *Oxford Book of Latin Verse*. And a more recent critic, H. A. Mason (in 1963) denies Juvenal any claim to moral seriousness; though ranking him high as a poet because he is 'a supreme manipulator of the Latin language.' One of Johnson's predecessors in the 'imitation' of this poem, the French poet Boileau (1636–1711), was evidently so puzzled by its tone that in transferring its actions to the Paris he knew he had to divide it into two poems. One of these introduces the character of 'surly Virtue' which Johnson took over for his *London*, and it is a serious treatment of political and moral scandals. The other is a hilarious extravaganza in which the 'je' of the poem is a Jacques Tati figure, swept half-demented through scenes of funeral and scenes of farce, losing his hat. The English reader is reminded of Byron's *Don Juan*. Johnson, mostly through his mouthpiece 'injur'd Thales' – sometimes thought to be modelled on his friend Richard Savage – tries to maintain a tone of angry seriousness throughout. His poem is bitterly partisan. It is a scathing attack on the regime of Sir Robert Walpole for domestic corruption and appeasement of Spain. But it engages only the hard and noisy side of Johnson the political publicist, not the melancholy sceptic about 'laws and kings.' In other ways it has a very strange effect. The use of the Juvenal material, so full of burlesque and extravaganza, for serious polemical purposes leads to incongruities.

> Here falling Houses thunder on your Head,
> And here a female Atheist talks you dead.

It is hard to know just how to take this. A bit of Juvenal plus a bit of real life?

    The Vanity of Human Wishes is also an 'imitation' of Juvenal (the tenth poem) but now Johnson has found the right form for his matter. With the aid of Shakespeare he achieves the tragic note he had failed to produce in *Irene*. The Wolsey passage (99–129) shows the depth of his poetic relationship to Shakespeare. Macaulay thought Juvenal did better in making us visualize the fall of Sejanus, but Johnson creates a drama of the mind. After 'At length his Sov'reign frowns' we see every thing through Wolsey's eyes. For Eliot 'Swedish Charles' was the greatest passage (192–222). Charles XII was a much discussed figure in Johnson's day, and the career Johnson describes was historically portentous; its catastrophe was the battle of Poltava (1709) which was to make Russia a great European power, as Stalingrad (1943) made her a world power. Johnson rises to the historic occasion with splendid solemnity and grand irony. Much has been said also in praise of the 'young Enthusiast' of Oxford, the best known passage of Johnson's poetry and a fine example of his power to invest a commonplace with reality and poignancy.

> Yet hope not Life from Grief or Danger free,
> Nor think the Doom of Man revers'd for thee.

Equal strength is shown in the contrasting Maupassant-like portrait of the old man (256–90). My own favourite is the last of the little dramas of the poem, less often quoted; a witty sermon to the 'Nymphs of rosy Lips and radiant Eyes'.

> Against your Fame with Fondness Hate combines,
> The Rival batters, and the Lover mines.
> With distant voice neglected Virtue calls,
> Less heard, and less the faint Remonstrance falls;
> Tir'd with Contempt, she quits the slipp'ry Reign,
> And Pride and Prudence take her seat in vain.
> In croud at once, where none the Pass defend,
> The harmless Freedom, and the private Friend.
> The Guardians yield, by Force superior ply'd;
> To Int'rest, Prudence; and to Flatt'ry, Pride.
> Here Beauty falls betray'd, despis'd, distress'd;
> And hissing Infamy proclaims the rest.

[33]

Boileau's tenth satire may have helped Johnson to paint that lively miniature of fashionable society. Here as elsewhere in the poem his abstractions translate readily into individuals, such as Pope gives us in his tale of Sir Balaam, or Crabbe in his versified short stories.

The total effect (unlike Robert Lowell's imitation of the source-poem, 1967) is one of magnanimity. *The Vanity of Human Wishes* contains some of Johnson's best poetry, but often it is too declamatory and too 'tinny': the ghost of Roman satire still haunts it. I feel that a successful satirist must be something of a buffoon; a grave satirist, such as Johnson, is almost a contradiction in terms. *Rasselas* remains his real masterpiece on this subject.

I think Johnson's best poems are the *Prologues*: 'Drury Lane', the prologue to Goldsmith's *The Good-Natur'd Man*, and above all the prologues to *Comus* and to Hugh Kelly's *A Word to the Wise*. Johnson has found the attitude to the audience that suited what he wanted to say to them. His contempt is balanced by his respect for literary and moral decency. We hear the voice of the great Johnson of the Preface to the *Dictionary*. Personal bitterness comes through, but so too does largeness of soul and, in the end, Christian humility. The prologue to *A Word to the Wise* is the greatest of these poems. Here the Johnsonian generality was an asset. He could not say anything about the play itself because he did not admire Kelly, so he appeals for English fair play and asks the audience to make a beautiful and ceremonious occasion out of a performance of something which in itself may have lacked merit. We hear Johnson's moral authority:

> To wit, reviving from its author's dust,
> Be kind, ye judges, or at least be just:
> Let no resentful petulance invade
> Th'oblivious grave's inviolable shade.
> Let one great payment every claim appease,
> And him who cannot hurt, allow to please.

Most of Johnson's later poetry is light verse, the bagatelles and throw-offs preserved by Mrs Thrale. Her character and her relationship with Johnson cannot be described briefly. On his side it appears to have been what psychoanalysts call a 'transference' relationship, and it may well have saved his life and sanity. The literary results were also happy. In his early poems Johnson had no Muse and he found it hard to create a convincing *persona*. Democritus, invoked in *The Vanity of*

Human Wishes, the man who laughs at everything, would not really do, for Johnson was a Tchehovian character, tragic as well as comic. But in his later poetry his Mistress was his Muse, and his *persona* is convincing: the gregarious Johnson, Johnson without his wig, who could be at home with topers as with fashionable ladies, with profligates as with scholars, a figure of Shakespearean largeness, humour, and charity.

This later verse consists mostly of what Johnson called 'Easy Poetry', one of his critical terms which, unlike 'Metaphysical Poets', has never been taken up. He defines it thus: 'Easy poetry is that in which natural thoughts are expressed without violence to the language. The discriminating character of ease consists principally in the diction, for all true poetry requires that the sentiments be natural.' I have found no discussion of Johnson's essay on Easy Poetry (*The Idler* 77), but I believe it to be crucial for the understanding of his later work. He was to say of the revolution in English poetry effected by Dryden that Dryden 'found it brick and left it marble', but here he seems to prefer 'brick'. He praises the directness of Cowley, an aspect of that poet at variance with the Metaphysical, fanciful aspect which Johnson deprecated. Johnson's conception of this kind of poetry resembles what W. H. Auden called 'Light Verse'. It will be seen that Johnson's view of this genre allows for its accommodation of the serious and even tragic.

Johnson had ceased to be a formal satirist by now, and we should think of him as an *improvisatore*. His finest poem of this kind is his 'Reply to Impromptu Verses by Baretti'.

> At sight of sparkling Bowls or beauteous Dames
> When fondness melts me, or when wine inflames,
> I too can feel the rapture fierce and strong
> I too can pour the extemporary song;
> But though the number for a moment please,
> Though musick thrills, or sudden sallies seize,
> Yet lay the Sonnet for an hour aside,
> Its charms are fled and all its power destroy'd:
> What soon is perfect, soon alike is past:
> That slowly grows which must for ever last.

Something could be said here of Johnson's relations with Baretti, the volatile Italian, once tried for murder, the most disliked figure (with the exception of Hawkins) in the Johnson circle. But the poem does not require biographical comment. Its mode, like that of Ben Jonson's 'fit of rhyme against rhyme', is paradox: in the form of an impromptu the poet exalts the product of slow and deliberate creation as alone imperishable.

'The Short Song of Congratulation', sardonic and Housman-like, gains by a biographical gloss: its message was well suited to the future husband of Letty Lade, ex-mistress of the highwayman Sixteen-string Jack. But it stands well by itself as an indulgence of the 'Restoration' side of Johnson's temperament. The best known of these personal poems is 'On the Death of Doctor Levett' (no. 98). It is perhaps less immediately appealing; it is formal rather than 'easy'. It is deeply moving for those who know Levet, the man 'obscurely wise and coarsely kind', the companion of Johnson's solitary mornings, who, Johnson said, was the only man he knew who got drunk from motives of prudence (his patients could only pay him in gin), whose manners were brutal, but not his mind. But to students attending only to the words on the page it has seemed chilly and artificial. Perhaps the moral is that Johnson's poems, like Cowper's, but unlike Blake's, require us to conjure up the intimate world they came out of. Only then can we appreciate the pathos of a line like: 'Our social comforts drop away.'

DR JOHNSON'S
DICTIONARY, 1755

ON SUNDAY, 10 OCTOBER 1779, Johnson told Boswell that 'Dodsley first mentioned to me the scheme of an English Dictionary; but I had long thought of it.' Dodsley's connection with Pope may have led to this suggestion, since Johnson alluded to Pope's list of English authors whose usage he thought proper to cite in a Dictionary, in his *Plan of a Dictionary*, 1747. The collapse in 1745 of Johnson's projected edition of Shakespeare had left him free to consider some alternative undertaking, and it is likely that Dodsley's suggestion was made about this time. Johnson drafted an outline statement of the work, 'A Short Scheme for compiling a new Dictionary of the English Language' (no. 30), the last page of which he dated 30 April 1746. This manuscript was circulated, and at least two readers made brief notes on it. Some time in the autumn of the same year Johnson rewrote his *Plan*, modifying a few details from the 'Short Scheme', and then a fair copy (no. 31) was made and again circulated to several readers, one of whom was Lord Chesterfield. They made notes on it and Johnson revised it again before sending it to the printer. The rather untidy nature of this manuscript led to a good deal of further rewriting in the proofs before the work was published at the beginning of August 1747, as *The Plan of a Dictionary of the English Language*, in the form of a printed letter to the Earl of Chesterfield, and signed 'Sam. Johnson' on the last page. This *Plan* served as an elaborate advertisement, but in the meantime work had begun on the *Dictionary* itself.

The contract with the booksellers was signed on 18 June 1746, and on the same day Johnson advanced three guineas (£3.15) to Francis Stewart, one of his assistants. Stewart's receipt states that he was to begin work from 'Midsummer next', presumably 24 June 1746. Employment of an assistant shows that work had started.

The draft of the *Plan*, and the published version of 1747, reveal sufficient familiarity with linguistic problems to show that Johnson had set about the practical work of reading through a wide range of books in order to select examples of particular usages which could then be employed as illustrative quotations. Although he made use of earlier dictionaries, especially Nathan Bailey's *Dictionarium Britannicum*, Johnson seems not to have started with a word-list and then hunted out examples of usage, but rather to have begun with a course of wide reading from which he collected samples of usage, and then to have developed the list of words and produced the definitions. This meant that his definitions grew from the usages of English writers, and that the quotations act as reinforcements of the definitions.

His procedure was to read through the books and, with a pencil, to underline those words which occurred in sentences which clarified the meanings of the word. He then wrote in the margin the initial letter of the underlined word, and marked off with vertical lines the beginning and end of the passage to be quoted. This made quite a mess of the books, and though they are highly valued today (only a dozen are known to exist), their condition was not appreciated by those from whom he might have borrowed them. The books he used were limited to the period from Shakespeare to Johnson himself. He did not concern himself with earlier English usage, nor with deliberately archaic language such as that of Spenser. He regarded the English language as having reached its highest degree of versatility and literary achievement during that period, and though it might have lapsed a little by adopting some French idioms and vocabulary at the Restoration, these were obvious aliens, easily identified and castigated.

Recent research has thrown new light on the procedures followed by Johnson and his assistants in the garret at Gough Square. Once Johnson had read and marked the book, it was handed over to the amanuenses. Their task was to transcribe the marked passages on to slips of paper and then to file the slips alphabetically under the appropriate word. When they had copied out the extract from the printed book, they crossed through the capital letter which Johnson had written in the margin, as an indication that they had completed the transcription. Each amanuensis had his own mark for crossing through the letter, so that it was possible to see which assistant was responsible for the slip bearing a particular extract under a particular word. This no doubt also facilitated payment. There were six copyists, and Boswell did not fail to notice that five were Scots:

two Messeurs Macbean; Mr Shiels, who we shall hereafter see partly wrote the Lives of the Poets to which the name of Cibber is affixed; Mr Stewart, son of Mr George Stewart, bookseller at Edinburgh; and a Mr Maitland. The sixth of these humble assistants was Mr Peyton, who, I believe, taught French, and published some elementary tracts.

It is clear that the slips would quickly accumulate, and that it would be necessary to control them from the start. From a very early stage, therefore, it is likely that there was an alphabetical file of illustrative quotations. It was Johnson's task to sift through them in order to eliminate redundancies, to select the most useful, and to arrange them in an order which would reflect the primary and subordinate senses of the words they exemplified. From his consideration of these examples evolved his definitions and classifications of the meanings of the words.

The *Plan* shows that it had been part of Johnson's purpose to make his *Dictionary* serve some of the functions of an encyclopaedia by selecting edifying quotations:

> it will be proper to observe some obvious rules, such as of preferring writers of the first reputation to those of inferior rank, of noting the quotations with accuracy, and of selecting, when it can be conveniently done, such sentences, as, besides their immediate use, may give pleasure or instruction by conveying some elegance of language, or some precept of prudence, or piety.

This purpose explains the drop-head title on the first page of the *Dictionary*: 'A General Dictionary of the English Language'. But by the time that the work was finished and the title-pages printed, the word 'General' had disappeared.

The work was printed by William Strahan, then of Little New Street, later to become the King's Printer, and founder of the firm now known as Spottiswood and Ballantyne. In the eighteenth century no printer could have held a stock of type sufficient to set up a book like the *Dictionary* as a single operation. It had to be done in instalments so that the type could be re-used. Strahan's account books have survived, and they show that by Christmas 1750, the first 70 folio sheets of volume 1 (including the first page with 'General' in the title) had been printed off. These sheets comprise the text from 'A' to 'Carry 21'. It is likely that this part of the work led both Johnson and the printer to realize that if they continued in the same proportion, the resulting book would be enormous, perhaps three or four large folio volumes, the cost of which and the consequent price would be exorbitant. The enterprise had to be retrenched. This is why the entries under the letters 'A' and 'B' are more expansive than under later letters, with cross-references, some of which (as under 'Aurora') lead nowhere. Johnson had to reconsider his principles of selection and pursue a more restrictive course in assembling his quotations and illustrating his definitions.

Strahan's printing accounts show that a further 50 sheets of volume 1 were printed by May 1752 ('Carry 22' to 'Dame 2') and there is little evidence in them of any significant reduction. It is likely that these slips had already been sorted and the printer's copy prepared before the problem of size became apparent. There is nevertheless, some evidence of optimism over his task on Johnson's part, for the bulk of the work of reading and selecting the quotations was nearly complete: in his *Rambler* 141 (23 July 1751), he had written: 'The Lexicographer at last finds the conclusion of his alphabet,' and it is perhaps not surprising to find him flexing his muscles with the threat of a strike against the proprietors in his letter of 1 November 1751, addressed to Strahan: 'my Resolution has long been, and is *not* now altered, and is now *less* likely to be altered, that I shall *not* see the Gentlemen Partners till the first volume is in the press . . .'

The death of his wife was a great distress and though his private journal noted his purpose on 6 May, after mourning, to 'return to life to-morrow', he was in November, still praying that he might so 'shun sloth and negligence, that every day may discharge part of the task which Thou hast allotted me', and on the 19th of the same month he composed a prayer 'After Time negligently and unprofitably spent'. These prayers reflect the end of a period of depression, and the *Dictionary* had been held up a little, for Strahan's records show that it was not until October 1753 that a further 100 sheets of volume 1 were printed ('Dame 2' to 'Grate'). Of course all would have had to be read in proof, and the disconnection of several catchwords shows that some significant changes were made at that stage by shifting passages about, or removing or introducing others. Though distressed, Johnson was not idle. His journals show that on 3 April 1753, he began work on volume 2, 'room being left in the first for Preface, Grammar & History, none of them yet begun.'

The work brought prosperity and business to Strahan who, on 1 November 1753, wrote to his American friend, David Hall, 'For this twelvemonth past I have employed seven Presses; and if I had had Room, could have kept two or three more'. Johnson's return to work was energetic enough to involve him with Mrs Lennox's pioneering study of Shakespearean sources, *Shakespeare Illustrated*, and he seems to have toyed with the preparation of a Collected Edition of his own works. At the end of 1753 there appeared the first *Index* to the first twenty volumes of *The Gentleman's Magazine* with a 'Preface' by Johnson, and a month later in

January 1754 he attended the death-bed of his old friend and employer, Edward Cave, founder of *The Gentleman's Magazine*, of whom Johnson wrote a short biography: 'One of the last acts of reason which he exerted, was fondly to press the hand which is now writing this little narrative.'

Strahan's affairs meanwhile continued to improve, and he had been busy enlarging his premises in Little New Street, on which he reported to Hall on 2 February 1754: 'My new House is compleatly finished, and I have at present Nine Presses going, which, you know, will do a great deal of Work.' These nine presses were working off the last instalment of the first volume of the *Dictionary*, some 56 sheets ('Grate' to 'Kyd'), which appears to have been finished early in 1754. Strahan's increased resources enabled him to plan the production of volume 2 much more efficiently, though by now the work which Johnson was sending in would also have been better organized. Strahan divided the work on volume 2 into sections by the letters of the alphabet, L–M, N–P, Q–R, S, T, U and V, and W–Z. These sections were apparently shared out among his compositors who were working on them simultaneously. If this was the pattern of the work, then Johnson must have completed the work of selecting, arranging, and defining the whole of the work from L to Z, and was occupied only in proof-reading and correction.

In the summer of 1754 Johnson visited Oxford, and the move to award him the degree of MA probably began. The printing of volume 2 was going forward in the autumn, and on 21 December he wrote to Thomas Warton at Trinity College: 'The Book cannot, I think, be printed in less than six weeks, nor probably so soon, and I will keep back the title-page for such an insertion as you seem to promise me.' The impediment to the completion of the work was perhaps not only the limitations of Strahan's shop, but also that Johnson had not yet written his 'Preface' and other preliminary essays, though his debt to John Wallis in the 'Grammar' may have been behind the summer visit.

Nevertheless the work was nearing completion, and in London the news reached the ears of the Earl of Chesterfield by whom the draft *Plan* had been read, and to whom the published version was addressed. Chesterfield had made a present of £10 to Johnson about that time, but thereafter made no further financial contributions or offered any other encouragement. Johnson had supported himself by hard work, and had received payment for the *Dictionary* work under the terms of the contract of 1746, which had stipulated a total of 1500 guineas (£1575). Chesterfield was an occasional writer, and on 28 November and 5 December 1754 two essays, heralding the approaching publication of the *Dictionary* were published in

The World. Though these essays were anonymous Johnson soon learned the identity of the writer. Their re-publication in *The Gentleman's Magazine* for December 1754 ensured a wider distribution, and Johnson had to consider what to do, since the implication of the essays was that Chesterfield had patronized the work all along. Having toiled virtually single-handed for some eight years, Johnson was not pleased. He gave the matter some thought, and, on 1 February, wrote to Thomas Warton, 'I now begin to see land, after having wandered, according to Mr Warburton's phrase, in this vast sea of words,' and on the 7th he addressed his famous rebuke to Lord Chesterfield. Though it is in the form of a private letter, Johnson regarded it as a public document and several versions are known.

> Seven years, My Lord, have now past since I waited in your outward Rooms or was repulsed from your Door, during which time I have been pushing on my work through difficulties of which It is useless to complain, and have brought it at last to the verge of Publication without one Act of assistance, one word of encouragement, or one smile of favour. Such treatment I did not expect, for I never had a patron before.

This matter out of the way, Johnson received, a fortnight later, the degree of MA from the University of Oxford which he had left after only fifteen months some twenty-six years before. He also probably revised his definition of 'Patron' in the light of his brush with Chesterfield. 'PATRON: One who countenances, supports or protects. Commonly a wretch who supports with insolence, and is paid with flattery.'

On 15 April 1755 the finished work was published in two large folio volumes, at £4. 10s. (£4.50) in boards. In the same month Strahan totted up his accounts, recording that he had printed 2000 copies, together with an octavo reprint of the *Plan* (still dated '1747') for a total of £1239. 11s. 6d. (£1239.57½). Although the sale of the whole edition should have recouped a total of £9000, the various shares of the proprietors, the protracted nature of the enterprise, and the extended investment, meant that, despite the high price, returns would be slow and unremarkable. It was therefore decided to publish a second edition in weekly numbers of alternately three and four printed sheets, at sixpence each. Part publication spread the cost to the purchaser who acquired a complete *Dictionary* after two years of subscribing a total of £4. 12s., and it provided an improved cash-flow to the publishers who also had a sensitive gauge to the market by which they could trim production to match any fluctuations in the sales. In fact demand for the second edition did slacken, and the number of copies of the weekly parts decreased as time went on, so that at the later stages only 768 copies were printed. This means that perfect copies of the second edition are much less common than copies of the first.

The proprietors of Bailey's *Dictionarium* perceived that their property was likely to lose in the face of the new competition, and they incorporated some of Johnson's material into a new edition which was then issued in parts to run concurrently with the second edition. Johnson's proprietors took legal advice only to find that their action would be too difficult to sustain. This competition from 'Bailey' may have contributed to the falling-off in demand for the second edition, but the proprietors had a further move to make, and they undertook an abridged edition in two octavo volumes which Johnson furnished with a brief 'Preface'. In this abridged version the illustrative quotations were omitted, and only the names of the authors were retained to show the authority of the usage. Strahan printed 5000 copies of this version in December 1755, and it was announced on 5 January 1756, at 10s. 6d. (£0.52½). The abridgement proved popular, and subsequent editions of 5000 copies each appeared at roughly five-yearly intervals for the next thirty years.

In 1765 there appeared a third folio edition of just over 1000 copies still at £4. 10s., and the proprietors' confidence in the work was such that they accepted a major revision of the *Dictionary* by Johnson and published it in 1773, still at the original price. For this work he received £300. The first break in this price-fixing came with the unauthorized Dublin quarto reprint in two volumes in 1775 from the revised fourth edition, but the London proprietors were not much disturbed and they issued 1000 copies of the fifth folio edition in 1784, still at the old price. This price maintenance was not broken until shortly after Johnson's death with the publication of quarto editions at nearly half the price.

Johnson's *Dictionary* remains a monument in English literary history because it still bears the stamp of an individual, and because it remains our only major dictionary compiled by a writer of distinction. Though the early retrenchment from an encyclopaedic approach may have been a disappointment to Johnson, it was really not uncongenial, for he was little interested in ordinary things, preferring to deal with ideas. Johnson is not much help to those who do not know what a cat or a mouse are ('CAT: A domestick animal that catches mice, commonly reckoned by naturalists the lowest order of the leonine species'. 'MOUSE: The smallest of all beasts; a little animal haunting houses and corn fields, destroyed by cats'). But he is an invaluable guide to the terms of economics, politics, literature and philosophy in the seventeenth and eighteenth centuries, and an acute discriminator of grammatical usages and nuances of meaning in everyday words: he offers sixteen definitions for 'In', over sixty for 'Make', nearly three columns on 'There', and its combined forms, and over twenty senses for 'Up'. Few earlier dictionaries had even tried to classify words in this way.

The range and variety of illustrative quotations, chosen by a single reader, give the *Dictionary* much of the flavour of an anthology. The total runs to something of the order of 116,000 extracts, and though the number used was far fewer than those originally chosen, most had been selected with a view to their edifying or literary quality. Any random sample will introduce the reader to a rich combination of extracts from the works of poets, historians, preachers, philosophers and scientists. Under the noun 'Light' for example, seven discriminated senses are illustrated by twenty-five quotations from Addison's *Spectator*, John Arbuthnot's *Table of Ancient Coins*, Bacon's *Natural History*, the Bible, Cowley, Dryden, Joseph Glanville, Hooker's *Ecclesiastical Polity*, John Locke, Milton, Newton's *Opticks*, Matthew Prior, Shakespeare, Robert South's *Sermons*, and Sir William Temple. Of these books only the Shakespeare and a volume of South's *Sermons* (no. 33) have survived.

Naturally, the definitions excogitated by Johnson himself as he sorted and reviewed the slips bearing the quotations, have attracted most readers to a sense of the compiler's particular qualities. Yet despite the presence of some marked idiosyncrasies it should not be forgotten that Johnson was compiling a dictionary of the *English* language, and not a collection of personal apophthegms larded with comments like Ambrose Bierce's *Devil's Dictionary* (1906). His purpose was to explain English words to English readers and to instruct them in their choice and use. The occasional quirks have been rather too much noticed at the expense of the solid, reliable accuracy with which English usage is described and distinguished. The personalities are well-known: 'Oats' contains a stroke at the Scots, 'Sublime' though a Gallicism, is reluctantly accepted, but 'Ruse' is dismissed as 'a French word neither elegant nor necessary'; Irish whiskey is preferred under 'Usquebaugh' to Scotch (he had not then visited Scotland), but 'Teague' kept the honours even. Under 'Grub-street', 'Lich', and 'Lexicographer' he allowed himself some freedom, and his wry comment on the last led to the single definition in later editions of Bailey as 'a harmless drudge'. The definitions of 'Cough' or 'Network' were seized upon as examples of verbosity, and the exactitude of his words was ignored. But it is not in these occasional surprises that the true strength of the *Dictionary* resides. The uncomplicated words which he supplied in his twelve definitions of a difficult word like 'Thought' show the fluent clarity of his own command of English:

1. The operation of the mind; the act of thinking.   2. Idea; image formed in the

mind.   3. Sentiment; fancy; imagery.   4. Reflection; particular consideration. 5. Conception; preconceived notion.   6. Opinion; judgement.   7. Meditation; serious consideration.   8. Design; purpose.   9. Silent contemplation.   10. Solicitude; care; concern.   11. Expectation.   12. A small degree; a small quantity.

And almost any everyday word will afford an equally striking example of Johnson's practical and businesslike command of English vocabulary.

As Adam Smith pointed out in his review of the first edition: 'Its merit must be determined by the frequent resort that is had to it. This is the most unerring test of its value . . . if a work of this nature be much in use, it has received the sanction of the public approbation' (*Edinburgh Review*, May 1755). Such indeed was the event, and Johnson's name became so far synonymous with the idea of an English dictionary that few were published thereafter which did not carry his name or portrait, no matter how remote their contents might be from his great work. Not everyone was pleased or satisfied with that work, and the growth of interest and skill in philology led to severe and valid criticisms, supplemented by learned and important publications, but the general reading public was unmoved: it had a dictionary on which it could rely, and Johnson remained the general foundation upon which English dictionaries stood until 1884 when there appeared the first fascicle of the *New English Dictionary*, edited by Sir James Murray.

Johnson's *Dictionary* was and remains a major achievement of his age. It almost realized that age's ideals of clarity and exposition, and it was not really superseded until those ideals had given way to others. Johnson contributed little to philology, and he had not much access to early forms of English; he was concerned with the written English of a particular historical period rather than the common speech, and he held a hierarchical view of linguistic propriety. These are no longer the values of dictionary-makers, and perhaps not of writers or readers, and Johnson remains as a striking monument to the aspirations of eighteenth-century English literary culture as well as to a remarkable personal achievement. As he observed to Boswell when the latter suggested that he had not fully realized what he was undertaking when he began the work, 'Yes, Sir, I knew very well what I was undertaking, – and very well how to do it, – and have done it very well.' Those words were no vain boast.

SAMUEL JOHNSON
CATALOGUE

by KAI KIN YUNG

1 · Lichfield, Oxford, and the Midlands

Johnson spent the first twenty-eight years of his life in the Midlands in total obscurity. A provincial bookseller's son, incomplete in his formal education, ungainly, weak in health but strong in spirit, he showed to those around him little signs of purpose or promise. His first inclination was to be a poet. He attempted translations, and experimented on themes closest to his heart.

1 · JOHNSON'S BIRTHPLACE, LICHFIELD, STAFFORDSHIRE
Clarkson Stanfield (1793–1867), 1835
Watercolour, $11\frac{1}{2} \times 9\frac{1}{4}$ in (29.2 × 23.5 cm)
Inscribed:
S! Mary's Church Town Hall
D! Johnson's House

In 1707, a year after his marriage, Michael Johnson (1656–1731) bought a house on the corners of Sadler Street and Breadmarket Street in Lichfield, Stafford-shire, demolished it and built a larger one. This imposing and spacious structure in the centre of the city, with ten rooms on the main floors, plus cellars and attic, was to be his shop as a stationer, bookseller, and bookbinder, as well as his home. He was bookish but at times melancholic, while his wife, Sarah Ford (1669–1759), from a yeoman family, was vain and condescending. 'My mother had no value for his relations; those indeed whom we knew of were much lower than hers.'

This view shows the market square in Lichfield almost as Johnson knew it, except for the absence of the market cross (or market house) which stood in front of the Birthplace until 1785. The drawing is from a series of twelve, specially commissioned by John Murray (1778–1843), the publisher, in 1835, for a revised and illustrated edition, to salvage the edition in 1831 by J. Wilson Croker of Boswell's *Life of Johnson*, which was condemned by the politically motivated review of Macaulay.

John Murray Esq

became 'a poor, diseased infant, almost blind' in the left eye, very near sighted in the other, and deaf in the left ear. In this condition and with parents not having had 'much happiness from each other', what Johnson remembered most with relish were his books and his exercises, exclusively in Latin, at Lichfield school from the age of about 7 to 16.

ANNALS: Histories digested in the exact order of time; narratives in which every event is recorded under its proper year.

Dr Johnson's House Trust

ANNALS.

1. 1709-10.

SEPT. 7*, 1709, I was born at Lichfield. My mother had a very difficult and dangerous labour, and was assisted by George Hector, a man-midwife of great reputation. I was born almost dead, and could not cry for some time. When he had me in his arms, he said, " Here is a brave boy †."

* 18 of the present stile. *Orig.*
† This was written in January, 1765. *Edit.*

2

2 · 'AN ACCOUNT OF THE LIFE OF DR SAMUEL JOHNSON, FROM HIS BIRTH TO HIS ELEVENTH YEAR, WRITTEN BY HIMSELF'
Richard Wright (editor)
London, Richard Phillips, 1805
Showing the beginning of 'Annals'

From internal evidence this account, of which the original manuscript is still untraced, may well have been written over a period of some ten years between 1763 and 1772, when Johnson was in his middle age. The ominous though factual beginning describing his difficult birth on 18 September 1709 is not surprising. His father was 52, and his mother 40. Through scrofula and other childhood illnesses he

3 · 'LINGUAE LATINAE LIBER DICTIONARIUS QUADRIPARTITUS (DICTIONARY IN FOUR PARTS OF THE LATIN LANGUAGE)'
Adam Littleton
London, 1678
Inscribed on front fly-leaf (by Johnson):
    Sam: Johnson/August 27th 1726
and on back fly-leaf (by Johnson):
    Sam: Johnson/Sept. 7th *1709* (O.S.) and
    1726
    1709
    ——
    17

One of four books extant owned by Johnson in 1726, all contributing to his classical education. Johnson's recording two dates in his Latin dictionary seems odd: the first obviously the date of his ownership; and the second calculating his age could hardly indicate a teenager conscious of mortality. Perhaps it was simply a mathematical curiosity. Having been, like his contemporaries, drilled hard in it, Latin remained for Johnson a language reserved for special and private expression. He used it in his diaries (especially on resolutions or recording the state of his health), prayers and meditations, personal poems (for example, on the stream at Lichfield where his father taught him how to swim, and on completing the 4th and revised edition of his

Dictionary), epitaphs on his immediate family and friends, and the famous salutation to his native city in his *Dictionary*:

> LICH: *Lichfield*, the field of the dead, a city in Staffordshire, so named from martyred christians. *Salve magna parens.*

Johnson Birthplace Museum (Lichfield City Council)

4 · HOLOGRAPH MANUSCRIPT OF 'UPON THE FEAST OF ST SIMON & ST JUDE'
Samuel Johnson

In the autumn of 1725 Johnson's 31-year-old cousin, the Rev. Cornelius Ford (1694–1731), invited him to stay at Pedmore, near Stourbridge. Stimulated by his knowledge and wisdom, Johnson stayed on until the following Whitsun. His Lichfield head-master therefore refused to take him back. Through Ford's help, Johnson entered the Stourbridge school in July 1726, as a student and assistant under the headmaster, John Wentworth. There he produced a number of exercises, all of which showed a marked degree of maturity for a boy of 16.

This poem was among the twelve sent to Boswell in November 1787 by William Bowles (1755–1826). Recognizing the commemoration of the two martyred saints on 28 October as one of the 'nobler themes', Johnson wondered, 'Where doth extatick fury move/My rude unpolish'd song.' He was, however, never to attempt anything similar again. 'Of sentiments purely religious, it will be found that the most simple expression is the most sublime.' He either put them in the condensed form of a Latin verse or, more privately, in his diaries. Ironically, the verse form, uncommon among all of his other poems, and used by poets before and during his times, was made more famous by his two friends for whose tragic lives he felt deeply: William Collins, in his 'Ode to Pity', and Christopher Smart, in his *Song to David*.

Anonymous lender

4

5

5 · LADY MARY WORTLEY MONTAGU'S
MANUSCRIPT ALBUM
Showing Lady Mary's transcript of Johnson's
'Friendship. An Ode', with a different title
'Ode on Friendship address'd To the Lady'

The precise date of composition of this poem is not
known, but is generally accepted as written at a
very early period, before Johnson's marriage in
1735. With variations, the poem was printed four
times during Johnson's lifetime, including its first
appearance in *The Gentleman's Magazine*, July 1743.
The fullest version, however, was contributed by a
'B.W.' after Johnson's death, to *The Gentleman's
Magazine*, in June 1785.

This transcript by Lady Mary Wortley Montagu
(1689–1762), after 1730, is the only one known of
Johnson's Ode in manuscript form. Like the version
in Anna Williams's *Miscellanies in Prose and Verse*
(no. 74) it curiously omits the following stanza
which reflects the melancholy mood of a young
man apprehensive of the harsh realities of human
relationships:

> Directress of the brave and just,
>> O guide me through life's darksome way,
> And let the tortures of mistrust
>> On selfish bosoms only prey.

The title in Lady Mary's transcript and the third line
in the first stanza (which should read 'To Men and
Angels only giv'n) suggest the poem was borrowed
by one of her friends or admirers perhaps to flatter
her. Since she was never in the Johnsonian circle,
two (or at the most, three) persons could qualify:
Richard Savage whom Johnson first met in London
in 1738, or Henry Hervey Aston who was in Lichfield
in 1730 and whose brother Lord John Hervey was
one of Lady Mary's intimate friends since the 1720s.

Johnson valued friendship throughout his life.
This sensitive and sincere tribute, with reference to
'kindred virtues' and 'sister souls' may well have
meant to refer to those who shared his interest,
including Edmund Hector (1708–94) and Cornelius
Ford, whose company he treasured most, in antici-
pation of his meeting new acquaintances and sur-
roundings at Oxford.

> ODE: A poem written to be sung in musick; a lyrick
> poem; the ode is either of the greater or less kind.
> The less is characterised by sweetness and ease; the
> greater by sublimity, rapture, and quickness of
> transition.

Harrowby Manuscript Trust

6 · PEMBROKE COLLEGE, OXFORD, WITH JAMES I
PRESENTING THE CHARTER TO LORD PEMBROKE,
THE FOUNDERS, AND BENEFACTORS
W. Green(e), *c.* 1743–4
Pen and ink and grey wash, $15\frac{1}{8} \times 18$ in
(38.3 × 45.8 cm)
Signed: *W. Greene delin.*
Inscribed on verso:
　Pembroke College/F. Dodd and *1744*

On 31 October 1728, after two years working in his
father's bookshop in Lichfield, Johnson entered
Pembroke College, Oxford, as a commoner (that
is, his tuition and lodging fees were paid). This was
made possible by a £40 legacy from an aunt who
died early in the year, and a promise of support
(sadly unfulfilled) by an old school friend. He had
brought with him over a hundred volumes, intending not so much to impress his fellow students, but

6

to be independent and concentrate on his studies.

Johnson's room was at the top of the tower, just above the gateway to the left of the picture. This drawing was executed by a 'W. Greene' who between 1733 and 1751 was employed to make designs for the Oxford Almanacks. It was engraved by George Vertue for the Almanack of 1744. Dr D. B. Brown, in his catalogue of *Early British Drawings* in the Ashmolean Museum, 1982, identifies the artist as the same 'William Green' who executed the painting of an Oxford booksale, formerly in the collection of the late Mr J. N. Bryson.

The Visitors of the Ashmolean Museum

7 · WILLIAM ADAMS, 1706–89
Joachim Smith (*c.* 1737–1814)
Wax medallion, oval $4\frac{1}{4} \times 3\frac{3}{8}$ in (10.8 × 8.5 cm)
Signed and dated: *JS/1763*
Inscribed on a label on the back of frame:
> *William Adams D.D./bapt. 1706; d.1789. Master of/Pemb. Coll. Oxford. Archdeacon of Llandaff./ He married Jan. 12 1742 Sarah, daughter of/ Thomas Hunt of Boreatton, Co. Salop, by whom he/left one daughter, Sarah, who married July 10,/ 1788, Benjamin Hyett of Painswick./Ben. Hyett dying s.p. and without relations left/Painswick Ho. to his wife's nearest relation, Wm. Henry/Adams (his first cousin once removed) who assumed the/ name of Hyett./This model is probably by Isaac Gosset the/elder (1713–1799) a well known modeller of/portraits in wax. The signature appears to/be 'I.G.1763' but it might be 'I.S.'*

A junior fellow at Pembroke when Johnson arrived, William Adams became the most loyal of a very small group of friends of Johnson at Oxford. Adams, however, widly romanticized Johnson's time there as 'the happiest part of his life'. He told Boswell that Johnson was 'a gay and frolicksome fellow' and 'was caressed and loved by all about'. In fact as Johnson said, to hide his poverty, 'I was rude and violent. It was bitterness which they mistook for frolick.'

When Adams returned to Pembroke in 1775 as Master of the College, after having variously been a curate, a prebend, and a rector in the Midlands, he was Johnson's principal host when the latter visited Oxford in his later years. In 1776, Johnson felt easy enough to recommend to Adams a total stranger, 'a learned Benedictine', 'to Pembroke College, to be shown that a lettered stranger is not treated with less regard at Oxford than in France'.

Private Collection

7

8 · 'A MISCELLANY OF POEMS BY SEVERAL HANDS'
Published by J. Husbands, AM
Oxford, 1731
Showing page 111, beginning of Johnson's translation of Pope's 'Messiah'

Written as a Christmas exercise in 1728 for his tutor, William Jorden (d.1739), Johnson's first published piece is a translation of Alexander Pope's 'Messiah' into Latin. Pope is said to have thought well of it; 'The writer of this poem will leave it a question for posterity, whether his or mine be the original.' The volume itself is, as the title promises, a college miscellany. For immediately following Johnson's serious attempt is a totally light-hearted poem, presumably by another undergraduate, 'On the Taking of a Mistress'.

The British Library (1484 h.7)

9 · HOLOGRAPH PAGE FROM JOHNSON'S DIARY AT OXFORD, OCTOBER TO 21 NOVEMBER 1729

This first page from Johnson's first extant diary opens with his characteristic determination 'I bid farewell to Sloth, being resolved henceforth not to

9

listen to her syren strains' (Boswell's translation). He had been in College for a year and was now resolved to study seriously the works of Lucretius, Velleius Paterculus, Justinus, and Graevius's edition of Tully's *Letters*. On 21 November, he set himself a mathematical table and calculated if by reading certain lines a day, how many he would have accomplished in a week (Sunday excluded), a month, or a year. When he reached between 150 and 600 a day, he realized the annual targets would be astronomical. Memorizing large chunks of literary works was no great challenging feat for him, and calculating his readings remained one of his favourite hobbies. 'Nothing amuses more harmlessly than computation, and nothing is oftener applicable to real business or speculative enquiries.'

The next entry in his diary, Johnson recorded the date of his departure, December 1729, not knowing he was never to return as a student.

DIARY: An Account of the transactions, accidents, and observations of every day; a journal.

Anonymous lender

10 · MRS ELIZABETH PORTER, AFTERWARDS MRS JOHNSON, 1689–1752
Unknown artist
Canvas, oval $29\frac{1}{8} \times 24$ in (74.3×61 cm) *sight*

Having taught very briefly in the early part of 1732 at Market Bosworth School, Johnson went to Birmingham at the invitation of Edmund Hector. He lived there for most of the next two years, working on his first book, a translation of Father Jerome Lobo's *Voyage to Abyssinia*, and contributing to *The Birmingham Journal*. He also met Harry Porter, a mercer and woollen draper, who died in September 1734. When Johnson, aged 25, married his widow, on 9 July 1735, Mrs Porter was 46, with three children between the ages of 10 and 18.

This portrait of Tetty, as Johnson used to call her, is believed to have been painted not long before their marriage. Johnson told Mrs Thrale, 'Her hair was eminently beautiful, quite blond like that of a baby; but that she fretted about the colour, and was always desirous to dye it black, which he very judiciously hindered her from doing.'

Anonymous lender

11 · 'THE GENTLEMAN'S MAGAZINE', JUNE 1736
Showing Johnson's advertisement for his boarding school

With his wife's financial assistance, and encouraged by his friend and patron, Gilbert Walmesley (1680–

1751, a lawyer and registrar of the ecclesiastical court of Lichfield) Johnson rented a substantial house where, as his advertisement in June and July in *The Gentleman's Magazine* says, 'At Edial, near Litchfield, in Staffordshire, young gentlemen are boarded and taught the Latin and Greek by Samuel Johnson.' Temperamentally unsuited and physically unappealing, Johnson again found himself a failure as a teacher of young boys. He attracted only a handful of pupils, among them the boisterous and mischievous David Garrick and his younger brother, George.

National Portrait Gallery, London

10

2 · First years in London

The hardest years for Johnson were also his most creative. For fifteen years he toiled as a journalist, published his first two major poems, saw his only play performed, embarked on his great *Dictionary*, and became known as the author of *The Rambler* – the essayist and moralist. He even contemplated an edition of Shakespeare's plays. 'No man but a blockhead ever wrote, except for money.' It was a remark made not so much in jest as to remind himself of a professional writer's basic need for survival, especially for him who had neither a degree nor useful connections.

An engraving by T. Worlidge after a portrait (now lost) by F. Kyte of 1740 was prefixed to *The Gentleman's Magazine* of 1754. This one by Grignon, of larger plate and more elaborate design, with a quotation from Milton's *Paradise Lost*, was probably executed for circulation among Cave's friends. Grignon was working for the *Magazine* in the 1750s.

MAGAZINE: Of late this word has signified a miscellaneous pamphlet, from a periodical miscellany named the *Gentleman's Magazine*, by *Edward Cave*.

National Portrait Gallery, London

12 · EDWARD CAVE, 1691–1754
Charles Grignon (1721–1810), *c.* 1754
Engraving, 10½ × 7¼ in (26.7 × 18.4 cm)

Born in Newton, Warwickshire, and educated at Rugby School, Cave, having had a few odd jobs including being a printer's apprentice and a miscellaneous writer, purchased a printing house in 1731 and became proprietor and editor of *The Gentleman's Magazine*. Shrewd and hardworking, he gathered around him a group of promising writers and poets. By 1738 his magazine had 'given rise to almost twenty imitations of it', and its success could only be matched by *The London Magazine*, which was 'supported by a powerful association of booksellers'. Johnson commented that Cave was slow, but added, 'He saw little at a time, but that little he saw with great exactness. He was long in finding the right, but seldom failed to find it at last.' And according to Hawkins, Cave had, contrary to his pen-name 'Sylvanus Urban', 'few of those qualities that constitute the character of urbanity'.

12

13 · SOUTH EAST VIEW OF ST JOHN'S GATE, CLERKENWELL

John Chessell Buckler (1793–1893)
Ink and watercolour, $6\frac{1}{2} \times 8$ in (16.5 × 20.3 cm)
Signed and dated: *J. C. Buckler 1809*
Inscribed below picture:
    South East View of St Johns Gate Clerkenwell

For fifty years the offices of *The Gentleman's Magazine* occupied the large room above the arch. In Cave's times, the gatehouse was also his residence. Beneath the arch there were two passages, one for vehicles and the other, smaller, for pedestrians. These were removed in 1771.

The Museum of the Order of St John

14 · 'THE GENTLEMAN'S MAGAZINE', MARCH 1738
Showing Johnson's first contribution,
'Ad Urbanum'

Johnson's first approach to Cave in November 1734 to 'undertake on reasonable terms sometimes to fill a column' brought no response. It was not until this

13

Latin poem, a defence of Cave against his attackers, was accepted that he began as a contributor to *The Gentleman's Magazine*.

For the next six years *The Gentleman's Magazine* was his chief source of income. While Cave 'would contract for lines by the hundred, and expect the long hundred', Johnson experienced to the full the 'tolerable livelihood' of a journalist and of writing rapidly and working under pressure. Varying his skills he contributed, besides poems and biographical sketches, mock parliamentary reports under the Swiftian title 'Debates in the Senate of Lilliput'. Johnson went to the gallery only once. But his imaginative powers were such that even though the speeches were concocted from hearsay they were for twenty years regarded by the general public as authentic.

> The Journalist, indeed, however honest, will frequently deceive, because he will frequently deceive himself. He is obliged to transmit the earliest intelligence before he knows how far it may be credited; he relates transactions yet fluctuating in uncertainty; he delivers reports of which he knows not the Authors. . . . All that he can do is to consider attentively, and determine impartially, to admit no falsehoods by design, and to retract which he shall have adopted by mistake.

National Portrait Gallery, London

15 · ELIZABETH CARTER 1717 –1806
Joseph Highmore (1692–1780)
Canvas $50\frac{1}{4} \times 40\frac{1}{2}$ in (127.6 × 102.9 cm)
Inscribed:

HIGHMORE PINX

Educated by her father, the Rev. Nicholas Carter, of Deal, Kent, and driven by her own determination, Elizabeth Carter could do almost anything she set her mind to. She could cook, sew, play the spinet or German flute, as well as translate French, Greek, and other languages. She was a contributor to *The Gentleman's Magazine* in her teens. 'Poor dear Cave,'

15

as Johnson wrote to her, 'I owe him much, for to him I owe that I have known you.' He was first attracted to her by her English riddle which appeared in the February issue of *The Gentleman's Magazine* in 1738. He wrote to Cave, 'I have composed a Greek Epigram to Eliza, and think she ought to be celebrated in as many different languages as Lewis le Grand.' Later, in August, Johnson contributed more verses entitled 'To Eliza plucking Laurel in Mr Pope's Gardens'. The opening stanza curiously anticipates this portrait of her:

> As learn'd Eliza, sister of the Muse,
>> Surveys with new contemplative delight
> Pope's hollow'd glades, and never tiring views
>> Her conscious hand his laurel leaves invite.

Dover District Council

16 · SIR JOHN HAWKINS, 1719–89
James Roberts (fl.1776–1809)
Canvas 30⅛ × 25⅛ in (76.5 × 63.8 cm)
Inscribed and dated:
S! J. Hawkins/1786

Hawkins first contributed to *The Gentleman's Magazine* in March 1739, and thus was one of Johnson's earliest friends in London. Himself a Londoner, and a tradesman's son, he rose gradually from being a lawyer in 1742 to a magistrate for the County of Middlesex in 1761. He was a man of varied interests and talents, and his edition of *The Complete Angler* (1760) was praised by Johnson as 'very diligently collected, and very elegantly composed'. As a musician and musicologist Hawkins knew Boyce and Pepusch, while his own masterpiece, *The History of Music* (1776), which took him sixteen years to complete, brought him many well deserved honours, including this portrait, requested by Dr Philip Hayes, Professor of Music, for Oxford. Judging by his daughter's comment, the picture was not liked by the family. He was 'painted as he never looked, dressed as he never dressed, and employed as he never was employed,' since he was holding what appeared to be 'one of the last new novels then printed'.

Penurious and at times brutal, Hawkins was the least popular of the Johnson circle, and the most 'unclubable'. Yet he remained one of Johnson's most loyal friends. 'Let me have the benefit of your advice, and the consolation of your company' was his last request.

Faculty of Music, Oxford University

17 · 'IUNII IUVENALIS ET AULI PERSII FLACCI SATYRAE'
Amsterodami, 1626
Inscribed:
This book was formerly the property of
Dr Samuel Johnson. It was given to me by
Dr Wright of Lichfield, who received it from

Frank Barber, Dr Johnson's servant whom he
attended in his last illness. Charles Nutt. Sep! 14ᵗʰ 1818
Showing title-page

Johnson, who had Juvenal's Satires 'all in his head', had no less than twenty-two copies listed in the Sale Catalogue of his Library (no. 108). The Satires of Juvenal and Persius were often bound together. This copy, given by the Johnsonian genealogist A. L. Reade to the Johnson Birthplace Museum, is bound with Martial's *Epigrams*, 1621. It is the only one known in existence as owned by Johnson. Being small, it was practical:

> Books that you may carry to the fire, and hold readily in your hand, are the most useful after all . . . a man will often look and be tempted to go on, when he would have been frightened at books of a larger size, and of a more erudite appearance.

Johnson Birthplace Museum (Lichfield City Council)

18 · HOLOGRAPH DRAFT OF 'LONDON'
Samuel Johnson
Inscribed by Johnson on verso:
London a Poem/publish'd May 12 1738

This draft contains 77 of the 263 lines of Johnson's poem, *London*. It includes the foreboding comment on night-time crimes in the metropolis, committed not just in the streets, but in the normally expected safety of a home:

> In vain these dangers past, your Doors you close,
> And hope the Balmy blessings of repose
> Cruel with guilt, and daring with despair,
> The midnight Murd'rer burst the faithless bar,
> Invades the sacred Hour of silent rest,
> And plants his Dagger in your slumbring Breast.

The sheet was originally folded, so the earlier section (lines 99–106, 148–50) are on the bottom right corner, with the last two lines being interpolation for the opposite page. The manuscript then continues as opened, from the top left corner.

Johnson's numbering of his lines (210, 248, and 260) does not correspond with the printed version and, being higher, implies that the original might have been longer.

Anonymous lender

19 · 'LONDON: A POEM, IN IMITATION OF THE THIRD SATIRE OF JUVENAL'
[Samuel Johnson]
London, R. Doddesley, 1738
Inscribed, by unknown hand: *by Samuel Johnson*
Showing title-page

L O N D O N:

A

P O E M,

In IMITATION of the

THIRD SATIRE of JUVENAL.

by Samuel Johnson

- - - - - - - - *Quis ineptæ*
Tam patiens Urbis, tam ferreus ut teneat se ?
JUV.

LONDON:
Printed for *R. Doddesley*, at *Tully's* Head in *Pall-Mall*.
MDCCXXXVIII.

19

In his first separately published poem, without his name, Johnson chose the fashionable form of imitation: 'a kind of middle composition between translation and original design', and joined the general attack on the ministry of Sir Robert Walpole. Beneath the racy language, and the impetuous youthful vigour of condemning the present and recalling the better past, Johnson's personal bitterness and frustration are quite clear,

By Numbers here from Shame or Censure free,
All Crimes are safe, but hated Poverty.

And Johnson was always ready to help the poor.

The poem brought him ten guineas (£10.50). Politically popular, it went into three editions in a year. Pope recognized the talent and said that the author 'will soon be déterré'.

A. D. Barker has more than convincingly argued that it was printed by Edward Cave's colleague, Thomas Gardner, and not Cave himself, by its topographical peculiarities, for example, 'R. Doddesley' instead of 'R. Dodsley' (see his 'The Printing and Publishing of Johnson's *Marmor Norfolciense* (1739) and *London* (1738 and 1739), *The Library*, 6th Series, vol. III, no. 4, Dec. 1981, pp. 287–304).

The British Library (162 n. 14)

20 · 'CATALOGUS BIBLIOTHECAE HARLEIANAE, IN LOCOS COMMUNES DISTRUBUTUS CUM INDICE AUCTORUM'
Five volumes
London, Thomas Osborne, 1743–5
Bookplate of: *Rev. T. Baker Whitbread*
Showing vol. 1, p. 3: Johnson's definition of the uses of catalogues in 'An Account of the Harleian Library'

In September 1742, Thomas Osborne, publisher and bookseller, purchased the great library of nearly half a million books, pamphlets, and manuscripts of the late Robert Harley, 2nd Earl of Oxford (1689–1741). To dispose of them Osborne employed his lordship's former secretary, William Oldys (1696–

An Account of the Harleian *Library.* 3

BUT the Collectors of Libraries cannot be numerous, and, therefore, Catalogues could not very properly be recommended to the Public, if they had not a more general and frequent Ufe, an Ufe which every Student has experienced, or neglected to his Lofs. By the Means of Catalogues only can it be known, what has been written on every Part of Learning, and the Hazard avoided of encountering Difficulties which have already been cleared, difcuffing Queftions which have already been decided and digging in Mines of Literature which former Ages have ex-haufted.

HOW often this has been the Fate of Students, every Man of Letters can declare, and, perhaps, there are very few who have not fometimes valued as new Difcoveries, made by themfelves, thofe Obfervations, which have long fince been publifhed, and of which the World therefore will refufe them the Praife ; nor can the Refufal be cenfured as any enormous Violation of Juftice ; for, why fhould they not forfeit by their Ignorance, what they might claim by their Sagacity ?

To illuftrate this Remark, by the Mention of obfcure Names, would not much confirm it ; and to vilify for this Purpofe the Memory of Men truly great, would be to deny them the Reve-rence which they may juftly claim from thofe whom their Wri-tings have inftructed. May the Shade at leaft of one great *Englifh* Critic reft without Difturbance, and may no Man prefume to infult his Memory, who wants his Learning, his Reafon, or his Wit.

FROM the vexatious Difappointment of meeting Reproach, where Praife is expected, every Man will certainly defire to be fecured ; and therefore that Book will have fome Claim to his Regard, from which he may receive Informations of the Labours of his Predeceffors, fuch as a Catalogue of the *Harleian* Library will copioufly afford him.

NOR is the Ufe of Catalogues of lefs Importance to thofe whom Curiofity has engaged in the Study of Literary Hiftory, and who think the intellectual Revolutions of the World more worthy of their Attention, than the Ravages of Tyrants, the Defolation of Kingdoms, the Rout of Armies, and the Fall of Empires. Thofe who are pleafed with obferving the firft Birth of new Opinions, their Struggles againft Oppofition, their filent Progrefs under Perfecution, their general Reception, and their gradual Decline, or fudden Extinction ; thofe that amufe them-felves with remarking the different Periods of human Knowledge, and obferve how Darknefs and Light fucceed each other, by what Accident the moft gloomy Nights of Ignorance have given Way to the Dawn of Science, and how Learning has languifhed and decayed, for Want of Patronage and Regard, or been over-

A 2   borne

20

1761) and Johnson, whose work he had known through the publication of Robert James's *Medicinal Dictionary* (no. 45) to prepare the catalogues. How the two men cooperated it is not known. But between them they produced two classic pieces of cataloguing, the Harleian Catalogue, and *The Harleian Miscellany of Pamphlets and Tracts* (1744–6) in eight volumes.

Although the task was, as Hawkins put it, 'not

above the capacity of almost the lowest of literary artificers', Johnson used the occasion to stress the importance of such a collection and indeed the value of the catalogue itself. To justify the unusual step of charging for it, Oldys and Johnson had to classify the entire collection, and occasionally supply notes on the authors and editions. In his 'Account of the Harleian Library', Johnson pointed out the rich-ness of the collection, from ecclesiastical and civil histories, ancient poetry, geography, physic, philos-ophy, criticism, to 40,000 engravings of Raphael, Titian, Guido, Nanteuil, and Hollar, and the 'great collection of original drawings'.

The small pamphlets and slim tracts were particu-larly vulnerable to decay or loss. In his *Proposals* for printing a selection from the vast collection of *Harleian Miscellany* of 350,000 items, Johnson listed no less than 140 varieties of subjects alphabetically from 'Admiralty Jurisdiction', 'Baths', to 'Voyages' and 'Witchcraft'. Their existence gave him the basis for his Preface to the *Miscellany* – a masterpiece on the history and development of the freedom of the English press.

Dr Johnson's House Trust

21 · AN ACCOUNT OF THE LIFE OF
MR RICHARD SAVAGE, SON OF THE EARL RIVERS
[Samuel Johnson]
The Second Edition
London, E. Cave, 1748
Showing pages 177–8, with Johnson's notes

Twelve years older than Johnson, Richard Savage already had had the 'golden part' of his life long before they first met about April 1738, as fellow contributors to *The Gentleman's Magazine*. Like Johnson, 'having no profession', Savage 'became by Necessity, an Author'. The poet of *The Bastard* (or so he claimed, as the illegitimate son of the Earl Rivers and the Countess of Macclesfield) was a wit, a great talker, a spender, and an obvious charmer who 'scarcely ever found a Stranger, whom he did not leave a friend'. Although now in dire straits, he fascinated Johnson.

Johnson's *Life of Savage* grew out of a year's intimate relationship with this extraordinary man before Savage left for Wales. He vividly recalled the times when Savage had no money for a room, 'walked about the Streets till he was weary, and lay down in the Summer before a Bulk, or in the Winter with his Associates in Poverty, among the

[177]

sometimes reproved by his Friends who found him surrounded with Felons; but the Reproof was on that as on other Occasions thrown away; he continued to gratify himself, and to set very little Value on the Opinion of others.

But here, as in every other Scene of his Life, he made use of such Opportunities as occurr'd of benefiting those who were more miserable than himself, and was always ready to perform any Offices of Humanity to his fellow Prisoners.

He had now ceased from corresponding with any of his Subscribers except one, who *Pope* yet continued to remit him the twenty Pounds a Year which he had promised him, and by whom it was expected, that he would have been in a very short Time enlarged, because he had directed the Keeper to enquire after the State of his Debts.

However he took care to enter his Name according to the Forms of the Court, that the Creditor might be obliged to make him some Allowance, if he was continued a Prisoner, and when on that Occasion he appeared in the Hall was treated with very unusual Respect.

But the Resentment of the City was afterwards raised by some Accounts that had been spread of the Satire, and he was informed that
A a some

[manuscript note] Pope letter in his Life by Berenhead

21

Ashes of a Glass-house'. This was Johnson's first attempt at a 'critical biography' in which he later was to excel: a combination of assessing an author's life and works, occasionally leading on to his own brand of general, moral observations, that became a mirror not only to the man on whom he was writing but to life itself. The praise he lavished on Savage may at times seem excessive. But he had no illusion of the truth of the man. 'The reigning Error' of Savage's life was, 'that he mistook the Love for the Practice of Virtue, and was indeed not so much a good Man, as the Friend of Good.'

This is Johnson's own copy, made up of sheets (not consecutive) of the first (1744) and second editions. It is bound with Johnson's copy of his *Life of John Philip Barretier*, 1744.

Glasgow University Library (BD. 20-i.41)

22 · 'MISCELLANEOUS OBSERVATIONS ON THE TRAGEDY OF MACBETH: WITH REMARKS ON SIR T. H.'S [SIR THOMAS HANMER'S] EDITION OF SHAKESPEAR. TO WHICH IS AFFIX'D, PROPOSALS FOR A NEW EDITION OF SHAKESHEAR [SIC.], WITH A SPECIMEN'
London, E. Cave, 1745
Bookplate of: *Thomas James Wise*

Having tried his talents as a journalist, poet, bibliographer, and biographer, Johnson felt ready to take on the challenge to edit Shakespeare. He chose *Macbeth* as a starting point for discussion. By demonstrating that in Shakespeare's times 'the doctrine of witchcraft' was 'at once established by law and by the fashion', Johnson argued that the poet could not be considered as 'condemned to write Fairy Tales instead of Tragedies'. But no sooner had his project been announced than it was halted by the bookseller, Jacob Tonson (d. 1767), who claimed ownership of copyright and threatened legal action.

Copies of this work, complete with the *Proposals* at the end, are very rare. This was once the property of the notorious collector and forger, T. J. Wise

MISCELLANEOUS
OBSERVATIONS
ON THE
TRAGEDY
OF
MACBETH:
WITH
REMARKS
ON
Sir *T. H.*'s Edition of *Shakespear.*

To which is affix'd,

PROPOSALS for a NEW EDITION
of *SHAKESHEAR*, with a SPECIMEN.

LONDON:
Printed for E. CAVE, at *St John's Gate*, and Sold
by J. ROBERTS in *Warwick-lane*. Price 1s.
M.DCC.XLV.

22

(1859–1937), who happily recorded his bibliolatrous
experience on the bookplate:

> BOOKS BRING ME FRIENDS
> WHERE'ER ON EARTH I BE,
> SOLACE OF SOLITUDE –
> BONDS OF SOCIETY.

The British Library (Ashley 933)

23 · 'A PAGE FROM THE HOLOGRAPH DRAFT OF
'THE VANITY OF HUMAN WISHES'
Samuel Johnson

This page, selected from the complete manuscript
draft of Johnson's most famous poem, provides an

23

example of his extraordinary memory and peculiar
mode of composition which he describes to Boswell,

> I have generally had them in my mind, perhaps
> fifty at a time, walking up and down in my room;
> and then I have written them down, and often,
> from laziness, have written only half lines. I have
> written a hundred lines a day. I remember I wrote
> a hundred lines of The Vanity of Human Wishes in
> a day.

[Manuscript facsimile in Johnson's handwriting]

THE
VANITY
OF
HUMAN WISHES.
THE
Tenth Satire of *Juvenal*,
IMITATED
By *SAMUEL JOHNSON*.

LONDON:
Printed for R. DODSLEY at Tully's Head in Pall-Mall,
and Sold by M. COOPER in Pater-noster Row.
M.DCC.XLIX.

24

Should no Disease thy torpid veins invade
Nor Melancholys Spectres haunt thy Shade
Yet hope not Life from Grief or Danger free,
Nor think the doom of Man revers'd for thee
Deign on the passing world to turn thine eyes
And pause awhile from Learning to be wise
There mark what ills the Scolar's life assail
Toil envy Want the Garret and the Jayl

Anonymous lender

24 · 'THE VANITY OF HUMAN WISHES. THE TENTH
SATIRE OF JUVENAL, IMITATED BY SAMUEL
JOHNSON'
London, R. Dodsley, 1749
Bookplate of: *Oliver Brett*
Inscribed: *E Gainey*
Showing title-page

Within each group of generally a hundred, the first
half of the line is neat, clear, and earlier, whereas the
second half is thicker, less tidy for want of space,
and therefore later.

The first ten lines are from the passage relating to
a scholar's life:

Should Beauty blunt on fops her fatal dart
Nor claim the triumph of a letter'd heart

Ten years had passed since his outrage at the injustice and hardship in London. With all her faults, the town, as he was to say later, 'is my element'. In reviewing his own experiences and drawing from examples from history, the poet pondered on the futility of human aspirations, for glory, power, wealth, recognition, beauty and passion. Only Christian virtues could help to sustain a 'healthful mind' and bring hope,

> With these celestial Wisdom calms the Mind,
> And makes the Happiness she does not find.

A masterpiece of its kind, the poem carried for the first time his name on the title-page. It earned him fifteen guineas (£15.75) from his publisher. It made no immediate or widespread impact. No separate edition was called for during his life.

Dr Johnson's House Trust

25 · 'IRENE: A TRAGEDY, AS IT IS ACTED AT
THE THEATRE ROYAL IN DRURY-LANE'
Samuel Johnson
London, R. Dodsley, 1749
Showing p. 65, beginning of Act V, scene ii

Started while running his boarding school at Edial and finished about a year later, Johnson's one and only play took twelve years to reach the stage, when David Garrick was manager of Drury Lane. Irene, a Greek beauty, is caught, though not herself involved, in a plot to murder the Sultan, and is finally executed by him. This near Eastern tale became a series of solemn debates of weak government, 'happy Land' of 'circulating Pow'r', ambition, Christian freedom, and wealth and luxury in Moslem captivity. In Johnson's sonorous verse-drama, 'declamation roars, and passion sleeps'. Despite a strong cast, including Mrs Pritchard, Mrs Cibber, and Garrick himself, it ran for nine nights, never to be performed again.

Basil Barlow Esq.

26 · ASSIGNMENT OF THE COPYRIGHT OF 'IRENE'
FOR £100, 8 SEPTEMBER 1749
Signed: *Sam Johnson*

As a literary enterprise and a bid for fame, *Irene* fell far short of Johnson's expectations. He bore his disappointment 'like a monument'. Financially, however, it had reaped for him the most lucrative reward so far for a single work. In all, he received just a few pounds short of £300, from the clear profit due to him for the performances and the copyright fee for the publication of the work.

The Pierpont Morgan Library, New York (PML 19058)

26

27 · 'THE RAMBLER'
[Samuel Johnson]
Two volumes
London, J. Payne, 1753
Bookplate of: *Ralph Payne*
Inscribed: *D. of Grafton/1782*
Showing the first page of no. 5, 'Meditation on Spring'

Designed to keep himself financially independent while his big project, the *Dictionary*, was in progress,

Johnson produced a series of twice-weekly essays from 20 March 1750 for two years. Of the 208 numbers, less than 7 were by others. The popularity of pamphlets and periodical essays was to ensure success. These essays gave Johnson's genius the occasion to ramble in serious and eloquent prose, clearing it 'from colloquial barbarisms, licentious idioms, and irregular combinations'. Consistently keeping to his principal purpose 'to inculcate wisdom or piety', the essays range over a wide variety of subjects, from moral essays on truth, punctuality, patience, to amusing portrait sketches, criticism on eighteenth-century fiction, biography, Milton's poetry, and accounts of the life of a prostitute.

Contrary to his belief that he had 'never been much a favourite of the public', Johnson, 'Auteur du Rambler' (as the title of the French translation of *Rasselas* in 1760 so describes him) was nationally and internationally known. Although, as Hawkins and Murphy reckoned, less than 500 copies were sold in a day, the essays were quickly reprinted in other monthly magazines as well as in many provincial papers.

The British Library (89 h.11)

28 · JOHN HAWKESWORTH 1715?–73
James Watson (*c.* 1739–90) after Sir Joshua Reynolds
Mezzotint $9\frac{7}{8} \times 8\frac{3}{4}$ in (25.1 × 22.2 cm)
London, James Watson, 1773

Modelling on Johnson's success with *The Rambler* (no. 27), Hawkesworth produced his series of twice-weekly essays, *The Adventurer*, 1752–4, with contributions from Johnson and his other friends. An able journalist and successor to Johnson's authorship of the Parliamentary Debates for *The Gentleman's Magazine*, he was likewise an excellent imitator of Johnson's style, an early friend and one of the original ten members of the first club organized by Johnson, 'with a disposition to please and be pleased'. It met weekly at 'the King's head, a famous beef-steak house, in Ivy-lane near St Paul's, every Tuesday

28

evening'. Hawkesworth's subsequent career, varied and at times shaky, as a journalist, poet, playwright, biographer and editor of Swift (highly praised by Johnson), and editor of Cook's *Voyages* (which brought him attacks from all sides), earned him the title of 'coxcomb' from both Johnson and Reynolds. Johnson, however, remained steadfast as his friend and attempted, though never completed, an edition of his works, including his poems which, Johnson thought, 'show the progress of his Mind, and of a very powerful mind'.

National Portrait Gallery, London

29 · 'A SERMON, WRITTEN BY THE LATE SAMUEL JOHNSON, LL. D. FOR THE FUNERAL OF HIS WIFE'
Published by the Rev. Samuel Hayes
London, T. Cadell, 1788
Bookplate of: *Oliver Brett*
Showing page 14, on the character of his wife

After a long illness Tetty died on 17 March 1752, three days after the last number of *The Rambler*. That Johnson's childhood friend, John Taylor, should refuse to use this sermon, having first refused to compose one himself, is hard to understand. Apart from the page shown, most of the eighteen-page sermon concerns the general Christian views of death, forgiveness, and immortality. Although some of the attributes might seem exaggerated to his friends, it was characteristic of Johnson to stress that 'it will ill become beings like us, weak and sinful as herself, to remember her faults, which, we trust, Eternal Purity has pardoned'. In his private prayers and meditations he was to remember her constantly. Thirty years later, he wrote,

> This is the day on which in 1752 dear Tetty died. On what we did amiss, and our faults were great, I have thought of late with more regret than at any former time. She was I think very penitent. May God have accepted her repentance: may he accept mine.

Dr Johnson's House Trust

(14)

to fcoff at goodnefs, nor her reafon to difpute againft truth. In this age of wild opinions, fhe was as free from fcepticifm as the cloiftered virgin. She never wifhed to fignalize herfelf by the fingularity of paradox. She had a juft diffidence of her own reafon, and defired to practife rather than to difpute. Her practice was fuch as her opinions naturally produced. She was exact and regular in her devotions, full of confidence in the divine mercy, fub-miffive to the difpenfations of Providence, ex-tenfively charitable in her judgments and opi-nions, grateful for every kindnefs that fhe re-ceived, and willing to impart affiftance of every kind to all whom her little power enabled her to benefit. She paffed through many months languor, weaknefs and decay, without a fingle murmur of impatience, and often expreffed her adoration of that mercy which granted her fo long time for recollection and penitence. That fhe had no failings, cannot be fuppofed: but fhe has now appeared before the Almighty Judge; and it would ill become beings like us, weak and finful as herfelf, to remember thofe faults which, we truft, Eternal Purity has pardoned.

Let

29

3 · Lexicographer

The various stages of Johnson compiling his most famous work, *A Dictionary of the English Language*, are chronicled by Dr J. D. Fleeman in his essay at the beginning of this catalogue. In addition to illustrating its process, this section shows three other dictionaries which Johnson had helped and encouraged.

> LEXICOGRAPHER: A writer of dictionaries; a harmless drudge, that busies himself in tracing the original, and detailing the significance of words.

30 · 'A SHORT SCHEME FOR COMPILING A NEW DICTIONARY OF THE ENGLISH LANGUAGE'
Samuel Johnson

This is the first page of Johnson's draft, consisting of nineteen leaves, and dated at the end, 'April 30, 1746', nearly two months before he signed the contract with a group of leading booksellers consisting of John and Paul Knapton, Thomas Longman and T. Shewell, Charles Hitch, Andrew Millar, and Robert Dodsley who first suggested the project. The draft was intended to help him and his publishers to grasp the scope and nature of the work. That this was to be a single-handed enterprise, without any intention of securing the support of patronage, is clearly indicated in the opening paragraph, which also mentions that the words chosen will not just be those 'usually termed polite'. His dictionary was intended for popular use.

Anonymous lender

31 · A PAGE FROM THE REVISED DRAFT OF 'THE PLAN OF A DICTIONARY OF THE ENGLISH LANGUAGE'
Unknown hand, with notes by Lord Chesterfield and Johnson

The original 'Scheme', revised and expanded to 45 pages, had now been copied out by a secretary for circulation to Johnson's friends. On Dodsley's suggestion it was shown to Philip Dormer, 4th Earl of Chesterfield (1694–1773), the distinguished and learned statesman, who inserted a few comments. On leaf 12 of the original 'Scheme', Johnson had selected for illustration the several senses of the word 'ground' in order to explain its usage from the basic, then to the consequential and the metaphorical. In the revised draft he had added another word, 'arrive'. The passage continues, in Johnson's handwriting, on the verso of the page now shown:

> to mention any observation that arises from the com[parison] of one meaning with another, as it may be remar[ked of the] word *arrive*, that in consequence of its original [and ety]mological sense, it cannot be properly applied but to [words signifying] something desirable, thus we say a man [arrived] at happiness, but cannot say without a mixture of irony, he arrived at misery.

Anonymous lender

32 · 'THE PLAN OF A DICTIONARY OF THE ENGLISH LANGUAGE; ADDRESSED TO THE RIGHT HONOURABLE PHILIP DORMER, EARL OF CHESTERFIELD; ONE OF HIS MAJESTY'S PRINCIPAL SECRETARIES OF STATE'
[Samuel Johnson]
London, J. and P. Knapton, T. Longman and T. Shewell, C. Hitch, A. Millar, and R. Dodsley, 1747
Showing p. 1 of the text

A copy of the earlier and much rarer state of the *Plan*, with the address to Chesterfield repeated on

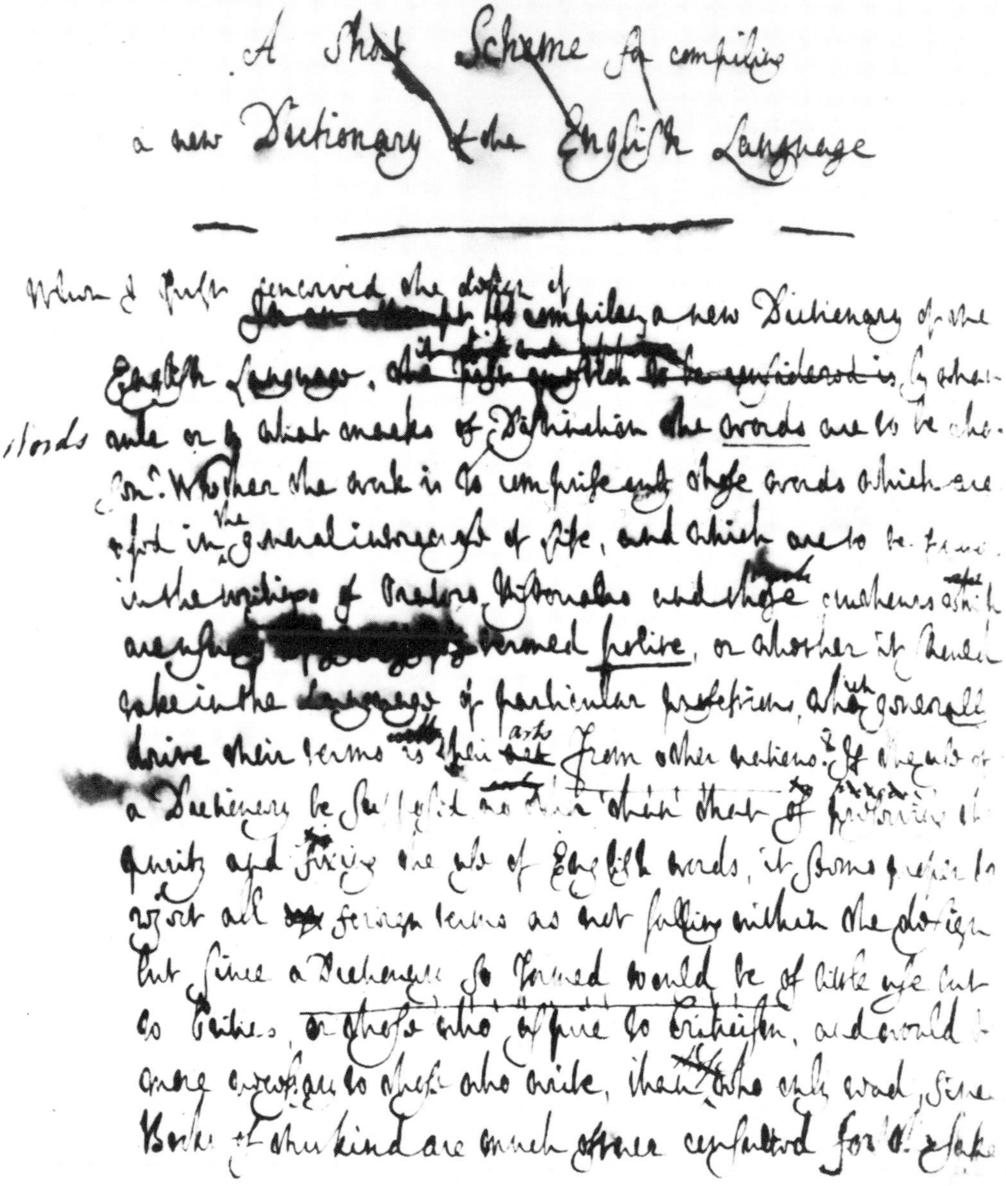

A Short Scheme for compiling
a new Dictionary of the English Language

When I first conceived the design of compiling a new Dictionary of the
English Language, it is first to be considered by what
rules or by what marks of distinction the words are to be chosen. Whether the work is to comprise only those words which are
used in the general intercourse of life, and which are to be found
in the writings of Orators, Historians and those authors which
are usually termed polite, or whether it should
take in the language of particular professions, which generally
derive their terms of art from other nations. If the end of
a Dictionary be supposed no other than that of preserving the
purity and fixing the use of English words, it seems proper to
reject all foreign terms as not falling within the design
but since a Dictionary so formed would be of little use but
to Critics, or those who aspire to Criticism, and would be
more necessary to those who write, than to those who only read, since
Books of this kind are much oftener consulted for the sake

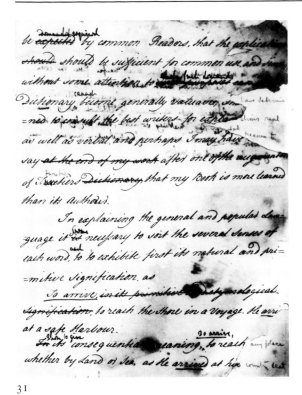

31

[1]

To the RIGHT HONOURABLE

PHILIP DORMER,

Earl of *CHESTERFIELD*;

One of His MAJESTY's Principal Secretaries
of State.

MY LORD,

WHEN firſt I undertook to write an Engliſh
Dictionary, I had no expectation of any
higher patronage than that of the proprietors of the copy, nor proſpect of any other advantage
than the price of my labour ; I knew, that the work
in which I engaged is generally conſidered as drudgery
for the blind, as the proper toil of artleſs induſtry, a
taſk that requires neither the light of learning, nor the
activity of genius, but may be ſucceſsfully performed
without any higher quality than that of bearing bur-
thens with dull patience, and beating the track of the
alphabet with ſluggiſh reſolution.

A   WHETHER

32

page 1. The other state, published in the same year, begins simply with 'My Lord'. In six long paragraphs at the beginning, Johnson seemingly complimented his patron. Proud that he had always been independent, he was not altogether sure of the effect or the outcome by dedicating his future work to Chesterfield.

> Not therefore to raise expectation, but to repress it, I here lay before your Lordship the plan of my undertaking, that more may not be demanded than I intend; and that, before it is too far advanced to be thrown into a new method, I may be advised of its defects or superfluities.

He was, in other words, requesting Chesterfield to pay some active attention to the progress of his work.

Basil Barlow Esq.

33 · 'TWELVE SERMONS, PREACHED UPON SEVERAL OCCASIONS'
Robert South
The Second Volume
London, Thomas Bennet, 1694
Inscribed:

(1) *This book was/given to me many/years since by/Ellen Jane, wife/of Richard Hinckley,/who by a former/husband was the/mother of the/Sleeping Children./The note on the/other side was/written by her./Frederick Hinckley,/17 Octr., 1883*
(2) *This book belonged to the late/Dr. Samuel Johnson. The/letters in the margin were/his writing and refer to the/marks in black lead pencil/in the pages. This was/the method he adopted/to form his Dictionary./I bought this Book/from Francis Barber's/Daughter.*

Showing pages 96 and 97

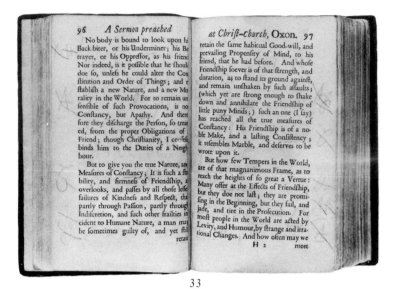

33

Of the vast number of authorities from philosophers, historians, scientists, writers, and poets, chosen by Johnson to illustrate the meanings of his words, only about a dozen are extant. This odd volume, made up of sermons by Robert South, and printed between 1664 and 1692, contains nearly 850 passages used by Johnson in his *Dictionary*. Johnson had underlined on pages 96 and 97 the words he wanted to use, marked the extent of his quotations, and further indicated his instructions with alphabets in the margins. From the variation of the strokes, one more horizontal than the other, possibly two amanuenses had done the copying. By the strokes they meant they had completed their task. The heavily marked pages are not surprising, since the subject of the sermon relates to friendship, and the text chosen is John, v. 15. Of the thirteen words selected, only 'indiscretion' and 'offer' are 'condemned to add the vexation of expunging', while 'underminer' is selected from another of South's sermons. The passages containing 'annihilate' and 'puny' have been appropriately reduced and altered, while the passage containing 'jade' and 'Prosecution' has been quoted in full.

Some passages I have yet spared, which may relieve the labour of verbal researches, and intersperse with verdure and flowers the dusty desarts of barren philology.

Dean and Chapter, Lichfield Cathedral

34 · HOLOGRAPH DRAFT FOR 'A GRAMMAR OF THE ENGLISH TONGUE'
Samuel Johnson

Towards the close of his essay on 'A Grammar of the English Tongue', printed at the beginning of volume 1 of the *Dictionary*, Johnson discusses versification in various measures. In this draft, written probably in 1755 when the *Dictionary* was nearly finished, he discovered his counting was at fault. To illustrate iambic measure, he had written 7 lines of trochaic measure, and for 2 trochaic lines of 6 syllables, he had given lines of 5. The crossed passages were, however, restored to their appropriate places in the printed version. Only the last four lines in this draft were omitted.

Anonymous lender

Versification is the arrangement of a certain number of Syllables according to certain Laws.

The feet of our verses are either iambick as alóft creáte, or trochaick as hóly lófty.

~~Our iam~~ Our iambick measures comprise verses —

— — — — — ~~of three Syllables~~

Here we may
Think and pray
Before death
Stops our breath
Other joys
~~Are but~~ toys.

of four. Syllables
With ravish'd ears
The Monarch hears.

of ~~five~~ Six
In the days of old
Stories plainly told

But when the ~~heav~~ hundredth year
Shall three times doubled be
Then shall an end appear
To all our Slavery.

The whole of this manuscript is in the handwriting of Dr Johnson
J. Graham

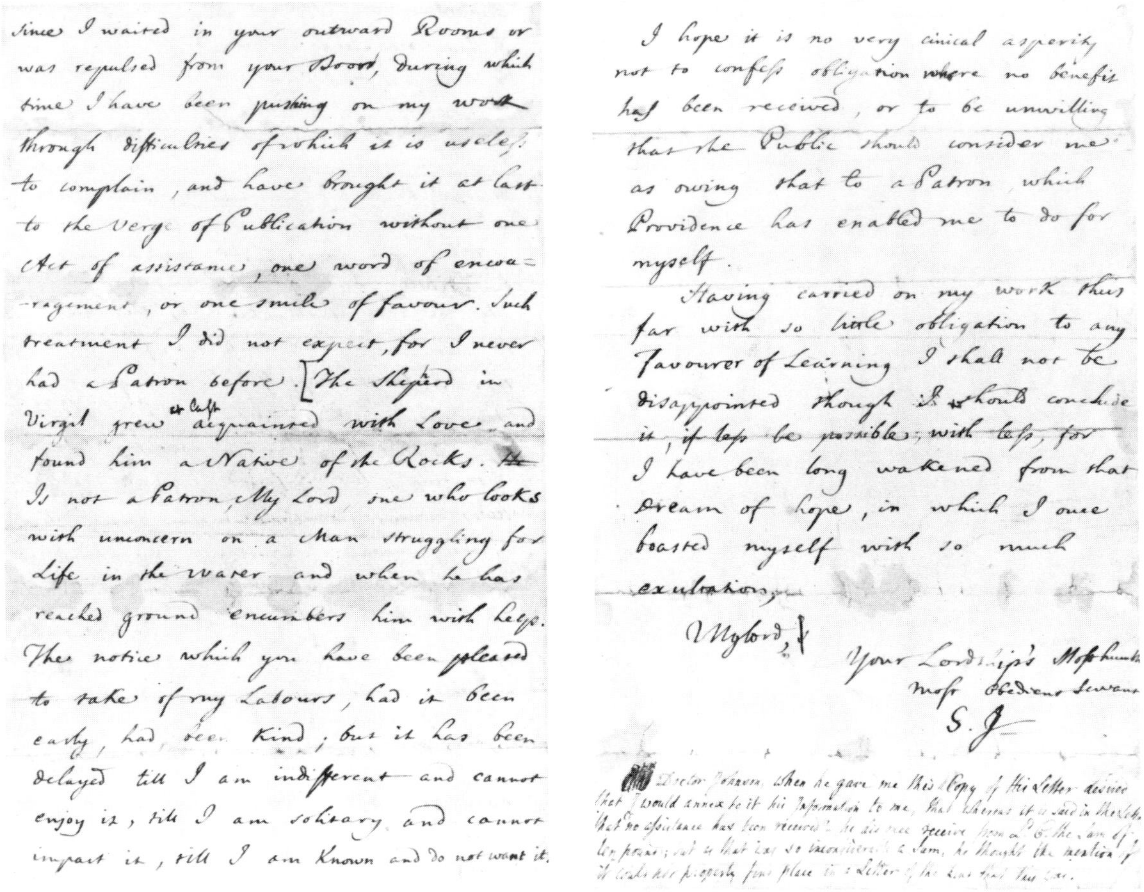

[facsimile of Johnson's handwritten letter, left page]

since I waited in your outward Rooms or was repulsed from your Doors, during which time I have been pushing on my work through difficulties of which it is useless to complain, and have brought it at last to the verge of Publication without one Act of assistance, one word of encouragement, or one smile of favour. Such treatment I did not expect, for I never had a Patron before. [The Shepherd in Virgil grew at last acquainted with Love, and found him a Native of the Rocks. Is not a Patron, My Lord one who looks with unconcern on a Man struggling for Life in the water and when he has reached ground encumbers him with help. The notice which you have been pleased to take of my Labours, had it been early, had been Kind; but it has been delayed till I am indifferent and cannot enjoy it, till I am solitary, and cannot impart it, till I am Known and do not want it.

35

[facsimile of Johnson's handwritten letter, right page]

I hope it is no very cinical asperity not to confess obligation where no benefit has been received, or to be unwilling that the Public should consider me as owing that to a Patron, which Providence has enabled me to do for myself.

Having carried on my work thus far with so little obligation to any Favourer of Learning I shall not be disappointed though it should conclude it, if less be possible, with less, for I have been long wakened from that Dream of hope, in which I once boasted myself with so much exultation. My Lord,

Your Lordship's Most humble Most obedient Servant

S. J.

35 · LETTER FROM JOHNSON TO
LORD CHESTERFIELD, FEBRUARY 1755
Dictated to Joseph Baretti by Johnson
Docketed (fl v) by Edmond Malone:

> Copy of D r Johnson's/Letter/to Lord Chesterfield;/ Corrected by himself, and/given by him to/Bennet Langton Esq re /see Dr Johnson's indorsement/on the back of p. 4/Presented to the British Museum/in June 1797, pursuant to the/intention of the late James Boswell Esq re /EM reconcinnavit 1794

Neither the £10 (as mentioned by Langton's note at the end of the letter) nor the two puffs by Lord Chesterfield, published in *The World* on 28 November and 5 December 1754, could be regarded as active support from a patron. Whatever the public might think did not trouble Johnson, but he himself could not commit, as he once accused Richard Savage of having done, 'literary hypocrisy'. He therefore chose to confront Chesterfield with the truth in the form of a letter. 'Seven years, my Lord, have now past', as he begins the third paragraph of his famous letter, 'since I waited in your outward Rooms or was repulsed from your Doors. . . .'

In his calculated, forceful language, Johnson asks, 'Is not a Patron, my Lord, one who looks with unconcern on a Man struggling for Life in the water and when he has reached ground encumbers him with help?' Chesterfield could hardly have missed the pointed imagery, on account of what Johnson had written about 'arrive' and 'ground' in the *Plan*.

The British Library (Add. MS. 5713)

36 · JOHNSON'S DIPLOMA AS MASTER OF ARTS OF OXFORD, 20 FEBRUARY 1755

The great work was near completion. A timely honour would be the degree of Master of Arts from his old university, which may 'grace the title-page of his Dictionary'. After some anxious negotiation from November 1754 by his friends Thomas Warton, fellow of Trinity College, and Francis Wise, Rad-

clivian Librarian, at Oxford, the Diploma was finally delivered to him on 25 February 1755.

The British Library (Add. MS. 38063)

37 · 'A DICTIONARY OF THE ENGLISH LANGUAGE'
Samuel Johnson
In two volumes
London, J. and P. Knapton; T. and T. Longman; C. Hitch and L. Hawes; A. Millar; and R. and J. Dodsley, 1755
Bookplate: GIFT FROM THE AUTHOR/TO/THOMAS SHERIDAN ESQR/F.R.I.A./1755
Vol. 1 showing pages from 'Acquisition' to 'Actitation'. The quotation from South's *Sermons*, using 'Act' as a verb, can be found under the 7th definition; Vol. 2 showing title-page

36

countrymen who felt excited with the new prospects in art and science, Johnson added a sense of confidence and pride in the richness of their native language.

> The chief glory of every people arises from its authours: whether I shall add any thing by my own writings to the reputation of *English* literature, must be left to time: much of my life has been lost under the pressures of disease; much has been trifled away; and much has always been spent in provision for the day that was passing over me; but I shall not think my employment useless or ignoble if by my assistance foreign nations, and distant ages, gain access to the propagators of knowledge, and understand the teachers of truth; if my labours afford light to the repositories of science, and add celebrity to *Bacon*, to *Hooker*, to *Milton*, and to *Boyle*.

Johnson Birthplace Museum (Lichfield City Council)

38 · WILLIAM STRAHAN 1715–85
Sir Joshua Reynolds, 1780–3
Canvas $35\frac{3}{8} \times 27\frac{5}{8}$ in (89.9×69.5 cm)

Strahan was born in Edinburgh, and came to London in the summer of 1738. By his diligence and shrewd business sense he quickly became one of the most prosperous printers and publishers. Printer of Johnson's *Dictionary*; he was also associated with most of his major publications afterwards, including *Rasselas*, *A Journey to the Western Islands of Scotland*, and the *Lives of the English Poets*. Strahan's other successes included Smollett's *Roderick Random* and *Peregrine Pickle*, part of Sterne's *Tristram Shandy*, Mackenzie's *Man of Feeling*, Adam Smith's *Wealth of Nations*, and Gibbon's *Decline and Fall of the Roman Empire*. He was the King's Printer in 1770, and an MP in 1774.

To Johnson, Strahan was a personal friend as well as a business associate. Financially unsystematic and frequently liberal towards the needy, Johnson was to find Strahan an invaluable manager, 'who was at once his friendly agent in receiving his pension for

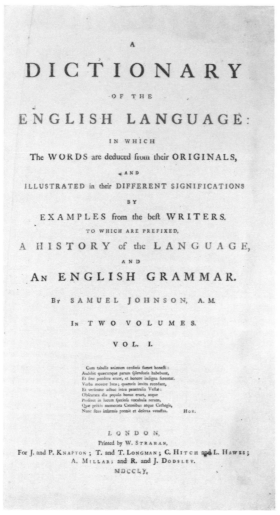

A
DICTIONARY
OF THE
ENGLISH LANGUAGE:
IN WHICH
The WORDS are deduced from their ORIGINALS,
AND
ILLUSTRATED in their DIFFERENT SIGNIFICATIONS
BY
EXAMPLES from the best WRITERS.
TO WHICH ARE PREFIXED,
A HISTORY of the LANGUAGE,
AND
AN ENGLISH GRAMMAR.
BY SAMUEL JOHNSON, A.M.
IN TWO VOLUMES.
VOL. I.

LONDON,
Printed by W. STRAHAN,
For J. and P. KNAPTON; T. and T. LONGMAN; C. HITCH and L. HAWES;
A. MILLAR; and R. and J. DODSLEY.
MDCCLV.

37

Not the first English dictionary, nor the first European one to use quotations to illustrate the meanings of words, Johnson's *Dictionary*, first published on 15 April 1755, is still an achievement uniquely its own. 'Language is the dress of thought.' It is more than a work of reference: the breadth of his knowledge, his wit and humour, and his comprehensive selections from the best authorities, have all made it a book for study and enjoyment. To his

38

39

him, and his banker in supplying him with money when he wanted it'.

This picture was exhibited at the Royal Academy in 1783, no. 230, and was first engraved by John Jones in 1792.

National Portrait Gallery, London (NPG 4202)

39 · SAMUEL JOHNSON 1709–84
Sir Joshua Reynolds, *c*, 1756
Canvas 50¼ × 40 in (127.6 × 101.6 cm)

The earliest known portrait of Johnson was and probably will always be a mystery in the absence of documentary evidence. Its early history before it was engraved in 1791 for Boswell's *Life of Johnson* is obscure, but it is generally believed to have been in the artist's collection ever since it was painted about 1756, after the publication of Johnson's *Dictionary*.

Reynolds left England in May 1749. He did not return to England from his Grand Tour until October 1752. In a memoir written by him about 1786 or 1787, he refers to his 'thirty years' intimacy with Dr Johnson'. Although Boswell hinted that the two men first met in 1752, the event could be as late as 1755 or 1756.

The portrait was cleaned and restored in 1976/7 and now represents the painting, more or less, as it was first executed. The design of a literary figure, seated, poised between moments of inspiration, with a quill in the right hand and papers or books on a table, is reminiscent of Rembrandt's painting of *The Apostle Paul* now in the Kunsthistorisches Museum, Vienna. The green tablecloth is characteristic of Reynolds in the 1750s and early 1760s.

No other versions, autograph or studio, are known. A miniature, now in a private collection and traditionally believed to be the earliest known portrait of Johnson, painted around 1736, and to have been worn by his wife as a brooch, is probably based on this painting. It shows a similar pose with part of the chair behind the figure. A reduced version in pastel, now in the Johnson Birthplace

Museum, could conceivably date around the late eighteenth or early nineteenth century.

National Portrait Gallery, London (NPG 1597)

40 · SAMUEL JOHNSON
James Heath (1757–1834) after
Sir Joshua Reynolds, *c*. 1790
Photograph of the First State of Engraving,
7⅞ × 5¾ in (18.7 × 14.6 cm)

Between the time the painting left the easel and this first state of Heath's engraving for the frontispiece of Boswell's *Life of Johnson*, published on 16 May 1791, certain changes had obviously taken place. The green tablecloth had been replaced by a wooden table, the left edge of the coat turned back, the waistcoat given six buttons, and the shape of the wig become more pointed at the top. An arm was added to the chair. Besides the paper on the table, there was a quill in an ink bottle; one large volume, clearly lettered 'JOHNSON'S ENGLISH DICTIONARY A-K'; and part of another volume. But who authorized these changes and when were they executed?

Mrs Bettina Jessell, in her 'Study of the paint layers of a portrait of Dr Johnson by Sir Joshua Reynolds PRA', published in the *Conservator*, No. 5, 1981, four years after she had finished cleaning and restoring the painting for the National Portrait Gallery, suggests that Boswell 'apparently employed a painter' to make these alterations, with the exception of the wooden table which, she thinks, 'was an attempt by a 19th-century owner to make the painting look more like an engraving after the portrait by Heath'. To do this would seem most unlikely, for Boswell had a great admiration for Reynolds, and to Reynolds he respectfully dedicated his book.

Readers of Boswell's *Life of Johnson* will be familiar with the following passage which appears just before the description of his first meeting with Johnson on 16 May 1763:

> I found that I had a very perfect idea of Johnson's figure, from the portrait of him painted by Sir

Joshua Reynolds soon after he had published his Dictionary, in the attitude of sitting in his easy chair in deep meditation, which was the first picture his friend did for him, which Sir Joshua very kindly presented to me, and from which an engraving has been made for this work.

From the context they are liable to imagine that Boswell had seen the picture before that date. In fact, Boswell did not meet Reynolds until September 1769.

In July 1786, Boswell began writing his *Life of Johnson*, and by January 1789 he had finished his rough draft. From then on he began revising until he delivered his Introduction to the printers on 1 January 1790. The manuscript of the *Life* is now at Yale University Library, and the rough draft for the above passage, which is on pages 207 and 208 reads originally:

I found that I had a very perfect idea of Johnson's
figure
~~appearance,~~ from a picture of him by Sir Joshua

Reynolds ~~which~~ in the attitude of sitting in his
          soon after he had published his Dictionary
easy chair in deep meditation ∧ which I believe was
                    for
the first picture his friend did ~~of~~ him. #
                produced
~~It has never been finished, though I cannot~~
~~help thinking~~
~~but think it a striking likeness.~~

Boswell normally wrote on the recto of a manuscript page, reserving the verso blank for later additions or alterations. On the verso of page 207 he has written:

                                        a present
          been so very good as to make me ∧
of which Sir Joshua has ~~kindly made~~

    # ∧ and from which an engraving has been made for this
work

From this draft and emendations the following conclusions can be drawn: (1) 'soon after he had published his Dictionary' was very likely based on an endorsement by Reynolds, since it was written in

40

a different ink and presumably later, (2) the picture 'has never been finished' before it was engraved, (3) an engraving was to be made for the book, (4) certain changes had to be and were made to the painting to make it look finished, which caused Boswell to cross out his original statement, and (5) Reynolds gave the picture to Boswell sometime during the year 1789 when Boswell's great work was approaching finish.

Although Reynolds had trouble with his left eye in July 1789, and by October had lost the sight of it, he continued to supervise the completion of his pictures, and might even have occasionally worked on them himself. To what extent the portrait of Johnson was 'unfinished' at the time is difficult to assess. Being the experimental painter that he was, it is even more difficult to say when and if he did or did not do certain things to his pictures. The ink bottle and quill, and the volumes (which were thought more finished than the rest of the painting and were therefore experimentally painted out during the conservation work in 1976/7) are common accessories in Reynolds's portraits of literary men of the mid-eighteenth century, and are therefore likely to be in the picture long before 1789, if not when it was first executed. A similar ink bottle with a quill sticking out at a strange and unbelievable angle can be seen in his portrait of Horace Walpole in 1756. It can also be seen in his second portrait of Johnson

of 1769 (no. 69). So to finish the painting before Heath began work on his plate, Reynolds probably supervised the covering of the green tablecloth with a wooden table, and the adding of the buttons to the waistcoat, if he did not actually paint them himself. The table could date from the 1750s.

Herman W. Liebert Esq.

41 · SAMUEL JOHNSON
James Heath after Sir Joshua Reynolds, *c.* 1790

41

Second State of Engraving, $7\frac{3}{8} \times 5\frac{3}{4}$ in
(18.7×14.6 cm)
Inscribed by Boswell below plate:

> *This is the first impression of the Plate/after M!*
> *Heath the Engraver thought it was/finished. He went*
> *with me to Sir Joshua Reynolds/who suggested that*
> *the countenance was too/young and not thoughtful*
> *enough. M! Heath/therefore altered it so much to its*
> *advantage that/Sir Joshua was quite satisfied, and*
> *Heath then saw such/a difference that he said he*
> *would not for a hundred/pounds have had it*
> *remained as it was.*

Heath was neither an experienced nor a first rate engraver. The first state of his engraving was unknown to Boswell. This second state which Boswell mistook as the first provides yet a few more interesting points: the eyebrows are longer and stronger; there are heavier shadows around the eyes; a corner of the chair has appeared behind Johnson's left shoulder (probably accidentally missed out by Heath in the first state); and there is an odd little shape which looks like a door handle between the left arm and the first volume of the *Dictionary*. (This last item is actually a smaller volume before it was experimentally painted out in 1976/7.) But Johnson still has a youthful and almost whimsical expression on his face.

Anonymous lender

42 · SAMUEL JOHNSON
James Heath after Sir Joshua Reynolds, *c.* 1790
Third State of Engraving, $7\frac{3}{8} \times 5\frac{3}{4}$ in
(18.7×14.6 cm)
Inscribed by Boswell below plate:

> *Second Impression of D! Johnson's Portrait/after*
> *the Plate had been improved by Sir/Joshua*
> *Reynolds's suggestions. M! Heath/afterwards gave*
> *it a few additional/touches.*

The engraving has by now, as Boswell says, 'improved by Sir Joshua Reynolds's suggestions.' The

42

eyebrows are even stronger than in the second state. A frown has appeared on the forehead. Heavier shadows around the eyes and the face have made it look slimmer. An arm has been added to the chair, supporting Johnson's right hand.

Anonymous lender

43 · SAMUEL JOHNSON
James Heath after Sir Joshua Reynolds
Fourth and Final State of Engraving, lettered
(Frontispiece to the first edition of Boswell's Life of Johnson, 1791), $7\frac{3}{8} \times 5\frac{3}{4}$ in (18.7×14.6 cm)
London, Charles Dilly, 1791

Heath's 'few additional touches' are not easy to discover. These may amount to giving the image clearer definition, such as around the area of the breeches and along the left edge of the coat. While Heath's task was now finished, it would be logical to assume that since Reynolds had suggested the alterations to the engraving, he himself had to see that the painting would match up. The last few touches he therefore probably authorized were connected with the ageing process to the face, and the adding of the arm to the chair. To publicize his book, Boswell released the news of the engraving to the public in an advertisement in *The London Chronicle*, 31 March 1791, announcing hopefully its publication 'in a few days', 'illustrated with the following plates: Dr Johnson by Heath from the large Picture painted by Sir Joshua Reynolds in 1756, being the first, and never before published.'

44

43

The painting remained in Boswell's family until the sale of his son's library on 3 June 1825, lot 3293, inaccurately described as 'painted for the late James Boswell, Esq. of Auchinleck'. It was bought by John Graves, a hop merchant, for 73 guineas (£76.65).

National Portrait Gallery, London

44 · PRELIMINARY SKETCH FOR THE
ILLUSTRATION TO CHAPTER I IN 'VANITY FAIR':
BECKY SHARP THROWING JOHNSON'S
'DICTIONARY' OUT OF THE COACH WINDOW
William Makepeace Thackeray (1811–63), *c.* 1847
Pen and ink $5\frac{1}{2} \times 4$ in (14 × 10.2 cm)

Becky Sharp and Amelia Sedley were about to leave the Academy for young ladies on Chiswick Mall. It was customary for the mistress, Miss Pinkerton, to award her choice pupil as a farewell present a copy of Johnson's *Dictionary*, accompanied with a 'pious and eloquent' letter to the parents. Unlike her friend Amelia Sedley, Becky Sharp, 'an articled pupil' whose parents were poor, was not qualified for one. But when the girls were about to leave, Becky Sharp was surreptitiously given one by Miss Pinkerton's good-natured sister, Jemima. To everybody's surprise and horror, Becky Sharp flung the book back into the garden just as the coach was driving off. Fortunately not a costly damage, the copy was just one of the abridged editions, costing 'only two-and-ninepence' (14p).

> There is nothing more dreadful to an author than neglect; compared with which, reproach, hatred, and opposition, are names of happiness.

Anonymous lender

45 · 'A MEDICINAL DICTIONARY'
Robert James (1705–76)
Three volumes
London, T. Osborne, 1743–5
Showing Vol. 1: Dedication to Dr Mead

Recent researches have shown that in helping this work by James, a school friend in Lichfield, Johnson had written the Proposals, and about twelve biographical sketches. He certainly wrote the Dedication to Richard Mead.

> To censure all dedications as adulatory and servile, would discover rather envy than justice. Praise is the tribute of merit, and he that has incontestably distinguished himself any publick performance, has a right to all the honours which the publick can bestow. To men thus raised above the rest of the community, there is no need that the book or its author should have any particular relation: that

the patron is known to deserve respect, is sufficient to vindicate him that pays it. (*The Rambler* 136)

The British Library (777 1. 14)

46 · 'A DICTIONARY OF THE ENGLISH AND ITALIAN LANGUAGE'
Joseph Baretti
Two volumes
London, C. Hitch and others, 1760
Showing Vol. 1: Dedication

The dedication to 'His Excellency Don Felix, Marquis of Abreu and Bertodano' was written by Johnson. Baretti says in the Preface that he had taken Johnson and Buonmattei as his guides in the composition of his grammars.

The British Library (1332 g. 2)

47 · 'A DICTIONARY OF ANCIENT GEOGRAPHY'
Alexander Macbean (d. 1784)
London, G. Robinson and T. Cadell, 1773
Bookplate of: *Despina Karadja*
Inscribed: *D. Karadja/March 6, 1916*

Johnson had written the Preface to this work which was designed for use in schools. He had earlier written to Edward Cave in support of a military dictionary for which Macbean had collected 'very good materials'. Nothing, it seemed, had come of it.

Macbean was one of Johnson's six amanuenses while compiling his *Dictionary*. But his lack of drive and purpose led Johnson to say to Fanny Burney:

> He is a Scotsman; he is a man of great learning, and for his learning I respect him, and I wish to serve him. He knows many languages, and knows them well; but he knows nothing of life. I advised him to write a geographical dictionary; but I have lost all hopes of his ever doing anything properly, since I found he gave as much labour to Capua as to Rome!

Dr Johnson's House Trust

4 · Widower

On 24 April 1752, over five weeks after the death of his wife, Johnson prayed that his affliction 'may awaken my conscience, enforce my resolutions of a better life'. During the next ten years he completed his *Dictionary*, finally contracted a new edition of Shakespeare, continued as a journalist, and wrote his only but ever-popular novel. Fame assured, and new friends made, his private circumstances were still far from comfortable.

48 · 'AN ACCOUNT OF AN ATTEMPT TO ASCERTAIN THE LONGITUDE AT SEA, BY AN EXACT THEORY OF THE VARIATIONS OF THE MAGNETICAL NEEDLE. WITH A TABLE OF VARIATIONS AT THE MOST REMARKABLE CITIES IN EUROPE, FROM THE YEAR 1660 TO 1860'
Zachariah Williams (1673?–1755)
London, R. Dodsley and J. Jefferies, 1755
Various notes by Johnson including inscription opposite half-title:

> *Zachariah Williams, died July 12, 1755, in his/ eighty third year*

While Johnson was busy compiling his *Dictionary*, his compassion was attracted by the poverty-stricken Zachariah Williams and his daughter, Anna. She was blind and he, aged 78, was thrown out in May 1748, of the Charterhouse, having been there for nearly twenty years as 'a poor brother pensioner'. A learned physician and scientist, Williams had not been able to fix himself at a profession. His misfortunes might well have provided material for the character of Polyphilus in *The Rambler*, no. 19, for whom Johnson mourns,

> Thus is this powerful genius, which might have extended the sphere of any science, or benefitted the world in any profession, dissipated in a boundless variety, without profit to others or himself! He makes sudden irruptions into the regions of knowledge, and sees all obstacles give way before him; but he never stays long enough to complete his conquest, to establish laws, or bring away the spoils.

Although this pamphlet gives Williams's name on the title, it was in fact written by Johnson, based on Williams's theory. Johnson gave this copy to the Bodleian Library during his visit to Oxford in the summer of 1755, and registered it in Bodley's catalogue.

Curators of the Bodleian Library, Oxford (4° BS. 729)

49 · ANNA WILLIAMS, 1706–83
Frances Reynolds (1729–1807)
Canvas $23\frac{7}{8} \times 19\frac{7}{8}$ in (60.6 × 50 cm)
Apparently inscribed before relining:

> *The friend of Dr. S. Johnson. The portrait of/ Ann Williams, a sketch by Miss Frances Reynolds,/ sister to Sir Joshua Reynolds. Mr. Northcote,/ R.A. said the portrait is a good likeness./ A^{bm}. Wivell, 1838./ Ann Williams was blind./ Formerly belonged to James Boswell, Esq.,/to George Thornecroft of Dunston, 1900.*

At first a regular visitor, then an inmate of Johnson's household after Tetty's death, Anna Williams was for over thirty years a housekeeper, and 'a sister' to him until her death. 'Had she had good humour and prompt elocution, her universal curiosity and comprehensive knowledge would have made her the delight of all that knew her.' But sometimes, 'she hates everybody'. And Johnson was, as Mrs Thrale says, 'really oftentimes afraid of going home'.

This portrait, which was engraved by E. Stalker

it was with the *Harleian Catalogues*, Johnson set out in clear, scholarly terms, his target and in so doing gave an authoritative definition of the duties of a Shakespearean editor and commentator. He was to 'correct what is corrupt, and to explain what is obscure'. Shakespeare, leaving no reliable edition,

49

in 1817, was once the property of Boswell. It was in the sale of his son James's library, on 3 June 1825, lot 3292, and was bought by a 'Heber' for 15 shillings (75p).

Dr Johnson's House Trust

50 · 'PROPOSALS FOR PRINTING, BY SUBSCRIPTION, THE DRAMATICK WORKS OF WILLIAM SHAKESPEARE, CORRECTED AND ILLUSTRATED BY SAMUEL JOHNSON, LONDON, JUNE 1, 1756'
J. and R. Tonson, J. Knapton, C. Hitch and L. Hawes, and M. and T. Longman
Showing title page

Johnson's literary status now established, Jacob Tonson withdrew his former threat and began negotiating an edition of Shakespeare with him. As

LONDON, *June* 1. 1756.

PROPOSALS

For PRINTING, by SUBSCRIPTION,

THE

DRAMATICK WORKS

OF

WILLIAM SHAKESPEARE,

CORRECTED AND ILLUSTRATED

BY

SAMUEL JOHNSON.

SUBSCRIPTIONS are taken in by

J. and R. TONSON, in the Strand; J. KNAPTON, in Ludgate-Street; C. HITCH and L. HAWES, and M. and T. LONGMAN, in Pater-noster-Row.

50

should be consulted 'by a careful collation of all the oldest copies'. He was to read 'the same story in the very book which Shakespeare consulted'. He would not, like his former editors, 'slight their predecessors'. Instead, 'all that is valuable will be adopted from every commentator, that posterity may consider it as including all the rest, and exhibiting whatever is hitherto known of the great father of the English drama'.

Nearly all the publishers listed on the *Proposals* are familiar names except 'M. Longman'. Thomas Longman (uncle of the T. Longman above) had died in June 1755. His place was taken by his widow, Mary, who died on 16 January 1762.

Birmingham Public Libraries

51 · AGREEMENT BETWEEN JACOB TONSON
AND SAMUEL JOHNSON FOR AN EDITION OF
SHAKESPEARE, 2 JUNE 1756
By unknown hand, with signatures of Tonson and Johnson
Docketed:

> *Agreement with Mr Johnson/for an Edition of/ Shakespeares Plays/8 volumes 8vo/June 2d/1756*

With copies of the *Proposals* ready for circulation, Tonson and Johnson now signed a contract on 2 June 1756. According to this, Johnson was to have 250 sets 'free of all costs and charges'. For any subscribers in excess of 250 he was to receive 1 guinea (£1.05) each. The subscription was 2 guineas (£2.10) each. When Hawkins congratulated him on 'being now engaged in a work that suited his genius', his reply was characteristically down-to-earth:

> I look upon this as I did upon the Dictionary: it is all work, and my inducement to it is not love or desire of fame, but want of money, which is the only motive to writing that I know of.

Johnson Birthplace Museum (Lichfield City Council) (MS 19/1)

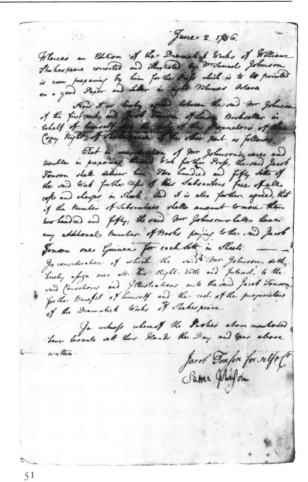

51

52 · AUTOGRAPH LETTER SIGNED, FROM JOHNSON
TO JACOB TONSON, 10 FEBRUARY 1758

His wife's funeral expenses, his amanuenses' fees for helping in the *Dictionary*, the mortgage repayment for his birthplace in Lichfield, and other domestic expenditure, had exhausted Johnson's literary earnings. Within three years he was twice arrested for debt, once in March 1756 and now, in February 1758. He appealed for help:

> The affair is about forty pounds. I think it necessary to assure you that no other such vexation can

happen to me for I have no other of any consequence but to my friends.

Johnson Birthplace Museum (Lichfield City Council) (MS 19/2)

53 · HOLOGRAPH PROMISSORY NOTE FROM JOHNSON TO JACOB TONSON FOR £40, 10 FEBRUARY 1758

The sum received, Johnson promptly issued this note, promising to pay 'on demand'.

Johnson Birthplace Museum (Lichfield City Council) (MS 19/3)

54 · 17 GOUGH SQUARE, FLEET STREET
John Crowther (born *c.* 1837)
Watercolour 8 × 6 in (21.3 × 17.1 cm)
Signed and dated: *J. Crowther – 1881*

Since his wife's death this house, leased by Johnson from about 1749, had been occupied by a new race of people. Anna Williams had brought her own furniture. A black boy called Frank Barber, from Jamaica, did the odd jobs. And a quack doctor, Robert Levet, probably came and went, though he had, according to Boswell, many years before he knew Johnson, 'an apartment in his house, or his chambers, and waited upon him every morning, through the whole course of his late and tedious breakfast.' The garret was like a counting house with desks when Johnson and his amanenses were working on the *Dictionary*. This Johnson considered as his library where, as witnessed by Reynolds and the sculptor, Roubiliac, on a visit:

> besides his books, all covered with dust, there was an old crazy deal table, and a still worse and old elbow chair, having only three legs. In this chair Johnson seated himself, after having, with considerable dexterity and evident practice, first drawn it up against the wall, which served to support it on that side on which the leg was deficient.

This drawing was one of a series commissioned by Sir Edward Hely Chadwyck-Healey (1845–1919) to record 'buildings and other features of the London scene which were either about to be demolished or likely to suffer such a fate at some future date.' It is the only one which has survived, of the many houses around Fleet Street where Johnson had lived for over fifty years.

Guildhall Library, City of London (Chadwyck-Healey c.1.13)

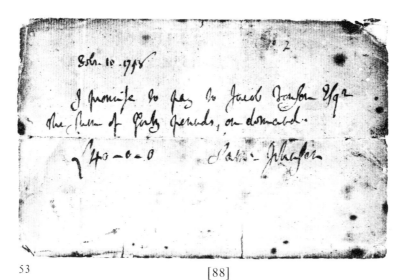

53

55

55 · CHARLES BURNEY, 1726–1814
Sir Joshua Reynolds, 1781, for Streatham Park
Canvas 29½ × 24 in (74.9 × 61 cm)

Organist, music teacher, and musicologist, Burney had seen with admiration Johnson's *Irene* at Drury Lane. He had been attracted by the 'learning and good taste' of *The Rambler*, and watched with excitement for news of the progress of the *Dictionary*. On the pretext of enquiring how to obtain copies for himself and his neighbours, Burney wrote to Johnson on 16 February 1755, expressing elaborately but carefully 'the pleasure and instruction' he had received from his 'admirable writings'. Johnson, who could easily dash off several letters in a day, took time to reply. He finally did, on 8 April 1755. In sincere terms, expressed beyond his usual code of courtesy, he told Burney that 'few consequences of my endeavours to please or to benefit mankind have delighted me more than your friendship thus voluntarily offered, which now I have it I hope to keep, because I hope to continue to deserve it.' He even invited Burney to write again and to let him know if he had found any faults with his *Dictionary*.

Their mutual literary interest kept them in contact, and Johnson's friendship extended to Burney's family, especially to his daughter, Fanny, the lively anecdotist of Johnson in his later years. For Burney, Johnson wrote the Dedication to the Queen for his famous *History of Music*, and three months before he died, the Dedication to the King for *The Commemoration of Handel* (published in February 1785).

In this portrait Burney is wearing his doctoral robes (Oxford 1769). It did not, however, impress Johnson. 'We want to see *Burney* and he never comes to me in that dress.'

National Portrait Gallery, London (NPG 3884)

56 · 'THE IDLER'
[Samuel Johnson]
Two volumes
London, J. Newbury, 1761
Bookplate of: *Oliver Brett*

Vol. 1 showing pp. 174–5, character of Mr Sober;
Vol. 2 showing title-page

Still threatened by financial worries, and the Shakespeare edition seemed far from finished, Johnson returned to the role of journalist. In a lighter vein, this series of humorous essays, collectively called *The Idler*, was designed for the common reader, not the learned, and to amuse, not to instruct. They were originally published as front-page essays in *The Universal Chronicle*, every Saturday, from 15 April 1758, with numbers running to 104, of which twelve are not by Johnson. The delightful character sketches, many of which were based on people he knew, are perhaps the most memorable. Their names betray their character: Dick Shifter, Tom Restless, Tom Tempest, Jack Sneaker, Will Puzzle, Ned Snuggle, etc. Peter Plenty complains that his wife is an auction hunter, 'Whatever she thinks cheap, she holds it a duty of an economist to buy. . . . She is always imagining some distant time in which she shall use whatever she accumulates.' Deborah Ginger wants her husband to return to his 'native element'. He has changed from a studious shop-keeper to a city wit, and is 'incessantly talking about liberty'. Dick Minim, the literary critic, 'did not trust so much to natural sagacity as wholly to neglect the help of books'. And Mr Sober's (Johnson himself) 'chief pleasure is conversation: there is no end to his talk or his attention; to speak or to hear is equally pleasing'.

Dr Johnson's House Trust

57 · 'THREE LETTERS TO THE IDLER'
[Sir Joshua Reynolds]
London, 1761
Signed inside cover:
(1) *Alg. P.S. Valentine*
(2) *D. Nichol Smith/Oxford, 1913*
Bookplate of: *Charles Meigh*
Inscribed on recto of endpaper:
*The following three/Letters were separately printed
off by Dr Johnson/for Sir Joshua Reynolds/and given*

by the latter/to M. *E. Malone in/1789 – /see Note*
facing/the Titlepage

Inscribed on fly-leaf by Edmond Malone:

Journal of a Scholar/by M. *Langton/Hacho King of*
Lapland – /Sam Softly – /and Journal of a/fellow of a
College/by the Rev. *Mr. Thos. Warton/These three*
*Letters/by S*ir *Joshua Reynolds./They were taken off*
by/Dr Johnson for S. *J.R./and this copy was given/*
by him to me Jan. 18, 1798/E. Malone

Showing Malone's inscription and title.

At the request of Johnson, Reynolds produced these three papers in 1759 for *The Idler*. He wrote on the 'False Criticisms of Painting', the 'Grand Style of Painting', and 'The true idea of beauty'.

This is one of two copies extant, with the three papers struck off and bound up especially. The other copy is at Yale University Library.

Curators of the Bodleian Library, Oxford
(Arch. A.f.115)

58 · SIR JOSHUA REYNOLDS 1723-92
Self-portrait, *c.* 1773
Panel 50 × 40 in (127 × 101.6 cm)

Reynolds's debut as a writer marks the early years of his long friendship with Johnson. It was one of mutual respect for each other's mind. Reynolds was captivated by the *Life of Savage* which he read on his return from Italy, and Johnson admired him for his 'habit of thinking for himself'. Although each had his own circle of friends, the closeness and import- ance of their relationship is best explained in this sincere admission from one of England's most res- pected portrait painters that for him Johnson had 'formed my mind and to have brushed off from it a deal of rubbish,' taking into account that among Reynolds's most penetrating character studies are those associated with the Johnsonian circle, includ- ing four of Johnson himself.

Johnson, in return, complimented Reynolds by quoting from his *Discourses* in the only revised (4th) edition of his *Dictionary* on no less than seventeen occasions under such words as 'genteelness', 'glow', 'nature', 'portrait', 'prospect', 'quietness', 'style' and 'tint'. He also wrote for Reynolds the Dedi- cation to the King in the first collected edition of the first seven *Discourses* in 1778.

In this self-portrait which shows Reynolds in his DCL gown (received from Oxford in July 1773) and painted in a style echoing Rembrandt, he is also alluding to the Grand Style of Painting by putting in the background the bust of Michelangelo, whom he called 'the Homer of painting'. The painting was a gift from Reynolds to the Royal Academy in 1780. It was engraved by Valentine Green in the same year.

The Royal Academy of Arts

59 · BENNET LANGTON 1737-1801
Unknown artist
Canvas 29¾ × 25 in (75.6 × 63.5 cm)

The eldest son of ancient landed gentry in Lincoln- shire, Langton was learned and pious. His one con- tribution to *The Idler*, even though it was probably polished up by Johnson, shows that he had a sense of humour. In this, modelling on Johnson's habits, he gives 'the Journal of a Scholar' who regrets at length the delays and interruptions which have prevented him from finishing his Essay, Treatise, Epic, and all kinds of studies.

Johnson introduced Langton to Boswell, and the two young men consolidated their friendship in their mutual object of interest, Johnson himself. Idle by nature, Langton was nevertheless generous and conscientious in helping Boswell and Hawkins in their works on Johnson.

Judging by the style of the wig and the costume, this portrait may date around the late 1770s, soon after Nollekens had finished his bust of Johnson which is in the picture. The strange pose and obvious admiration of Johnson may even indicate a self- portrait since Langton could paint.

Johnson Birthplace Museum (Lichfield City Council)

59

60

60 · THOMAS PERCY 1729–1811
William Dickinson (1746–1823) after
Sir Joshua Reynolds
Mezzotint $13\frac{1}{4} \times 10\frac{7}{8}$ in (33.7 × 27.6 cm)
Published 2 February 1775

Armed with a volume of manuscripts (as referred to in this engraving) containing old ballads found in a friend's house and saved from destruction by a maid intending to use it 'to light the fire', and other publishable material, Percy came to London in March 1759 to seek Johnson's advice in securing a prospective publisher. This meeting formed the real basis of their friendship, and from it came the legendary three volumes of Percy's *Reliques of Ancient English Poetry*, which appeared in 1765. Johnson helped with the glossary, refined the Dedication, and gave 'many valuable hints for the conduct of the work'.

A grocer's son, a scholar, especially of antiquities,

a cleric who rose to become chaplain to the Duke of Northumberland, then to the King (1769), Dean of Carlisle (1778), and finally Bishop of Dromore in Ireland (1782), Percy was obviously a man who had learned to tread his path cautiously. The 'Penantian' controversy which grew out of a discussion in April 1778 of a book, during which Percy and Johnson differed, put a check to their relationship. Basically cool-hearted, Percy took too much care not to offend. Johnson, who enjoyed goading his opponents in conversation, always understood a joke as a joke. In any case their friendship would probably never have reached the same degree of intimacy as Johnson's did with others such as Reynolds, Boswell, and Mrs Thrale.

National Portrait Gallery, London

61 · 'THE PRINCE OF ABISSINIA. A TALE'
[Samuel Johnson]

[94]

Two volumes
London, R. and J. Dodsley, and W. Johnstone, 1759
Bookplate of: *S. Adams*
Inscribed below bookplate:
  From the Author
Vol. 1 showing pp. 40–41, a discussion of flying, its invention and effect;
Vol. 2 showing title-page, with bookplate and inscription opposite

By January 1759, Johnson realized that his mother, whom he had not seen since 1740, was dying. Committed to *The Idler* essays, and reluctant to take the long journey to Lichfield, Johnson turned instead to the practical problems. The outcome was the publication in April of his only novel, written to 'defray the expence of his mother's funeral, and pay some little debts which she had left'.

The Prince of Abissinia, better known as *Rasselas* (meaning a chief), is one of Johnson's most significant works, for it embodies much of his philosophical interpretations of imagination, poetry, science, and marriage, and his humour and wisdom is richly redolent in numerous clear and moral precepts. Frequently translated, it has had over 400 editions since its first appearance. It is also a favourite with all Johnson's friends. Boswell admits that 'I am not satisfied if a year passes without my having read it through.'

This copy was probably among the parcel of books ordered by Johnson just before his death for delivery to William Adams at Pembroke College, Oxford. 'S. Adams' is either Adams's wife or daughter, both called Sarah.

Basil Barlow Esq.

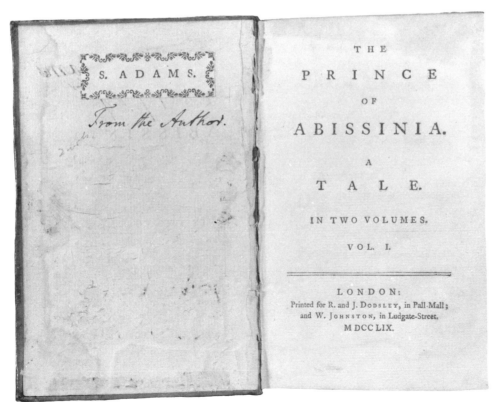

61

62 · 'A MEMENTO OF DR SAMUEL JOHNSON COM-
PRISING A LOCK OF HIS HAIR, THE AUTOGRAPH
MANUSCRIPT OF A PRAYER COMPOSED BY HIM,
AND TWO AUTOGRAPH LETTERS, ONE EARLY IN
HIS CAREER AND THE OTHER SHORTLY BEFORE
HIS DEATH'

Bookplate of: *R. B. Adam*

Inscribed by R. B. Adam:

*To/the Johnson Club/of London/from R. B. Adam/
Septr. 4th 1928*

Showing part of an autograph prayer by Johnson
on 'Scruples', *c.* 1759

Two other small fragments of this manuscript prayer
are extant, in a private collection. The sizes of all
three pieces are almost identical in width, indicating
perhaps that the manuscript was cut up to satisfy
several collectors. The word 'Amen' in the piece
now shown is not written by Johnson.

One further fragment exists in the Tinker Collection at Yale University Library. Unlike the other
fragments it is written on both sides of the paper,
which is almost half an inch wider. This is probably

taken from a notebook, and is from a transcript by
Johnson, dated 26 June 1768. The transcript is printed
in full in J. Wilson Croker's edition of Boswell's
Life of Johnson, 1831, Vol. V, p. 444. It reads as
follows:

Scruples

O Lord, who wouldst that all men should be
saved, and who knowest that without thy grace
we can do nothing acceptable to thee, have mercy
upon me. Enable me to break the chain of my sins,
to reject sensuality in thought, and to overcome
and suppress vain scruples; and to use such diligence
in lawful employment as may enable me to support myself and do good to others. O Lord, forgive me the time lost in idleness; pardon the sins
which I have committed, and grant that I may
redeem the time mispent, and be reconciled to thee
by true repentance, that I may live and die in peace,
and be received to everlasting happiness. Take not
from me, O Lord, thy holy spirit, but let me have
support and comfort for Jesus Christ's sake. Amen.

The editors of the Yale edition of Johnson's *Diaries,
Prayers, and Annals*, 1958, point out that the essence
of this prayer is so close to that of Easter Day, 15
April 1759, that the two are probably connected.
Johnson's inability to suppress sensual fantasies at
Easter distressed him deeply, and he felt all the more
repentant and the need of divine power to help him
'to support myself and do good to others.'

The two autograph letters of Johnson mentioned
as contained in this 'Memento' are: (1) to James
Elphinston, 20 April 1749, and (2) to George Nicol,
8 June 1784. In the front doublure is a miniature of
early twentieth-century workmanship, copied from
Opie's portrait of Johnson (no. 99). This and the
elaborate binding by Sangorski and Sutcliffe were
presumably commissioned by P. M. Pittar. The
'Memento' was included in the sale of his library
after his death, at Sotheby's on 4 November 1918,
lot 366, and again on 17 December 1919, lot 134.

SCRUPLES: Doubt; difficulty of determination;
perplexity; generally about minute things.

Dr Johnson's House Trust

5 · Pension, Boswell, and The Club

Johnson's circumstances improved considerably when, just before his 53rd birthday, he was awarded an annual pension by the King. He founded The Club with Reynolds, travelled widely with his friends, and began visiting the Midlands almost annually. In 1765, he received from Dublin his first honorary doctorate, and ten years later, his second, from Oxford.

63 · AUTOGRAPH LETTER SIGNED, FROM JOHNSON TO LUCY PORTER, 24 JULY 1762

Some of Johnson's friends thought that his literary achievements deserved recognition and, to alleviate his financial burden, his name should be included in the pension list. An anonymous letter, now established to have been written by Edward Blakeway, a Cambridge friend of Thomas Percy, was actually sent to the Earl of Bute, the new king George III's chief minister, in November 1761, stating that as a 'truly great author', Johnson 'deserves every reward that this nation can bestow on him'. When the offer of the pension was finally made informally to him in July 1762, Johnson hesitated on its acceptance. The lexicographer had previously defined 'pension' as 'an allowance made to any one without an equivalent. In England it is generally understood to mean pay given to a state hireling for treason to his country.' His friends convinced him that the reward was given solely on account of his achievements as an author, without any political motives. He therefore did not need to consider it improper to accept.

Five days after he had seen Lord Bute, Johnson wrote to his step-daughter in Lichfield to tell her the good news.

The John Rylands University Library of Manchester (Eng MSS 343/44)

64 · JAMES BOSWELL 1740–95
George Willison (1741–97), 1765
Canvas $52\frac{1}{4} \times 37$ in (132.7 × 94 cm)

The son of a Scottish judge and eighth laird of Auchinleck, Boswell arrived in London in November 1762, 'all life and joy', determined to be an officer in the army. A firm believer in the full enjoyment of life, which often reduced him to misery, he was also a lively and true recorder of it. 'I have therefore determined to keep a daily journal in which I shall set down my various sentiments and my various conducts.' With astonishing energy he hunted out great men, pursued women, travelled widely, and was soon to try his hand as an author.

His first meeting with Johnson at the back parlour of Thomas Davies's bookshop in Covent Garden on 16 May 1763, was hardly encouraging:

BOSWELL: 'Mr Johnson, I do indeed come from Scotland, but I cannot help it.' JOHNSON: 'That Sir, I find is what a very great many of your countrymen cannot help.'

But Johnson quickly warmed to his flamboyance and spirit of adventure, and Boswell was resolved to 'mark what I remember of his conversation'.

Scottish National Portrait Gallery (804)

Dear Madam

If I write but seldom to you, it is because it seldom happens that I have any thing to tell you that can give you pleasure, but last Monday I was sent for by the chief Ministre the Earl of Bute, who told me that the King had empowered him to do something for me, and let me know that a pension was granted me of three hundred a year. Be so kind as to tell Kitty. I

July 24. 1762

Dearest Madam
your most affectionate
Sam: Johnson

63

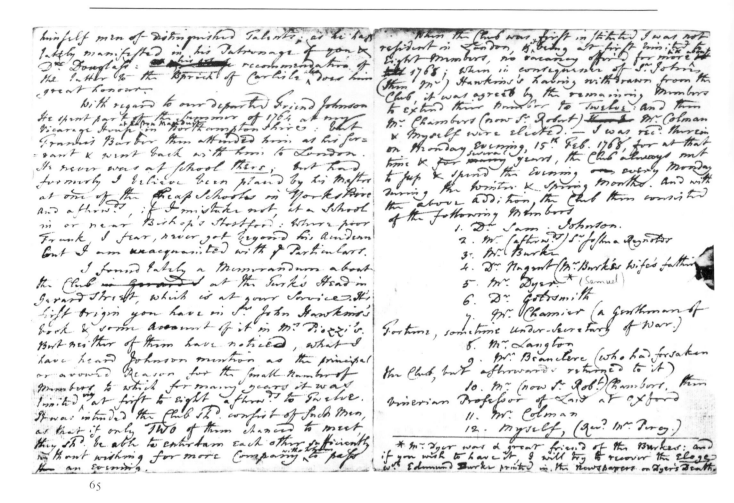

65

65 · AUTOGRAPH LETTER SIGNED, FROM THOMAS
PERCY TO JAMES BOSWELL, 28 FEBRUARY 1788

In answer to Boswell's enquiry, Percy wrote this
account of the origin of The Club, founded by
Reynolds, 'to which Johnson acceded'. Neither Mrs
Thrale (afterwards Mrs Piozzi) nor Sir John Hawkins had noticed, as Percy writes:

> what I have heard Johnson mention as the prin-
> cipal or avowed Reason for the Small Number of
> Members which for many years it was limited viz
> at first to eight afterw^{ds} to Twelve. It was intended

the Club sh^d consist of Such Men, as that if only
Two of them chanced to meet, they sh^d be able to
entertain each other sufficiently without wishing
for more Company with whom to pass an evening.

Percy mentioned 1764 as the year The Club was
founded, but did not give a date. In a note in his
engagement book now in the Royal Academy,
Reynolds refers to a dinner at '3½ Turk's Head' on
the afternoon of 16 April for the first time. This is
probably the date concerned.

Although this letter was folded and sealed, it was
probably not sent since it bears no postmark. A

revised version dated 29 February 1788, with postmarks 'MR3, MR 7 88', is in the Yale University Library.

Anonymous lender

66 · LIST OF MEMBERS OF 'JOHNSON'S CLUB – ACCORDING TO SENIORITY'

Since the list mentions the names of Thomas Warton and Adam Smith, the former being dead and the latter not, it must have been written after 21 May and before 17 July 1790. The unknown hand

66

who compiled this was obviously not closely familiar with the members ('Dr Scott' at the top right corner and 'Sir W. Scott' on the bottom line are the same man, and Johnson was spelt 'Johnstone'). The number, originally nine, had been increasing, and by 1780 it had reached thirty-five. Writing to his friend and fellow member, Sir Robert Chambers, in Calcutta, in April 1783, Johnson complained that 'the present state of the club, which is now very miscellaneous, and very heterogeneous it is therefore without confidence, and without pleasure.'

Anonymous lender

67 · EDMUND BURKE 1729–97
Studio of Sir Joshua Reynolds
Canvas $29\frac{3}{4} \times 24\frac{3}{4}$ in (75.6 × 62.9 cm)

Writer, orator, and statesman, born in Dublin, Burke went to London in 1750, first to study law but soon gave it up for writing and politics. His extraordinary intellectual power, as revealed in his popular treatise on the *Origin of our Ideas of the Sublime and the Beautiful* (1757), and his reputation as a conversationalist brought him into the circle of Johnson, Reynolds, and Garrick. He was one of the nine original members of The Club.

Referring to Burke becoming an MP and to his edition of Shakespeare being attacked, Johnson wrote to Langton in March 1766:

> Burke is a great man by Nature, and is expected soon to attain civil greatness. I am grown greater too, for I have maintained the newspapers these many weeks, and what is greater still, I have risen every morning since Newyears day at about eight, when I was up, I have indeed done but little, yet it is no slight advancement to obtain for so many hours more the conscious of being.

The original of this portrait was painted between 1767 and 1769. A mezzotint by James Watson was published in June 1770.

National Portrait Gallery, London (NPG 655)

67

68

68 · OLIVER GOLDSMITH 1728–74
Sir Joshua Reynolds, 1772, for Streatham Park,
version of the original painted about 1769 and
now at Knole
Canvas 30 × 25¼ in (76.2 × 64.1 cm)

Goldsmith, as Johnson commented, was a plant
'that flowered late'. But 'he always seemed to do
best that which he was doing'. By the time he knew
Johnson in the early 1760s, he was already the well-
known author of *The Chinese Letters* or *The Citizen
of the World*.

Reynolds called him a 'man of genius', but added
that 'others pronounced him an idiot inspired'.
Goldsmith was perhaps somewhere between the
two. With his extravagance (usually for him it
meant generosity to those who did not really need
it) and sense of fun, he endeared himself to Reynolds
and Johnson who attended the first night of his
She Stoops to Conquer. Johnson wrote the Prologue

to *The Good-Natured Man*, helped Goldsmith
with *The Traveller* and, after his death, composed
the celebrated Latin epitaph. The Club, of which
Goldsmith was an original member, commissioned
and erected a marble monument to him in Westminster Abbey.

*The Marquess of Tavistock and Trustees of the
Bedford Estates*

69 · SAMUEL JOHNSON
Sir Joshua Reynolds, 1769
Canvas 30 × 25⅛ in (76.2 × 63.8 cm)
Inscribed:
    SAM. JOHNSON. LD. OB! 1784
Inscribed on reverse:
    (1) *Sam! Johnson LD./anno aetat.60/
    J Reynolds – Pinxt. 1769*
    (2) *Purchased by His Grace/John Fred.ᵏ Duke
    of Dorset – 1769-*

69

This, and Reynolds's portrait of Goldsmith (the prime version of no. 68), were purchased by the Duke of Dorset as portraits of leading literary men. The two pictures are referred to in a technical note in Reynolds's Ledgers of 10 July 1769, 'Dr Johnston & Goldsmith 1st olio after Capivi with colori/but without white. The hand of Goldsmith cap. and white.' The portrait of Johnson may be earlier if it can be connected with the 'Mr Johnson' recorded in Reynolds's Sitters Books on 12 August 1765, 20 and 24 December 1766, 10 January and 18 April 1767, and 27 April 1769. On first impression the portrait looks idealized: the toga, scroll, quill, volumes, and sculptural profile. The original conception might well have derived from a detail from Raphael's classical composition, *Disputa* or *The School of Athens*. By its commonly known title *Dr Johnson Arguing* it is in fact misleading since Johnson is not in argument with anyone but is mentally wrestling with himself. The strange gesture is, however, not contrived. Both Reynolds and his sister had noticed Johnson's peculiar gesticulations. Reynolds noticed that when

> Johnson was left out of the conversation, either from his deafness or from whatever cause, he remained but a few minutes without speaking or listening. His mind appeared to be preying on itself; he fell into a reverie accompanied with strange antic gesticulations.

His sister, Frances, also noticed that,

> as for his gestures with his hands, they were equally as strange; sometimes he would hold them up with some of his fingers bent, as if he had been seized with the cramp, and sometimes at his Breast in motion like those of a jockey on full speed; and often would he lift them up as high as he could stretch over his head, for some minutes.

A studio variant, painted originally for Johnson's step-daughter, Lucy Porter, is now at Harvard University. It appears to have been overcleaned at some stage. It shows a less squinting right eye, blue instead of hazel as in this, with the cloak almost saffron in colour. Its background is dark greyish-blue, which would have been the ground layer before Reynolds added his 'capivi' (or copaiba balsam which is deep brown). The ones in the Tate Gallery and in the National Portrait Gallery are but copies, the latter being of the head only, painted on very finely machine-woven canvas of the mid-nineteenth century.

A mezzotint by James Watson was published on 10 July 1770.

The Lord Sackville

70 · EDMOND MALONE 1741–1812
Sir Joshua Reynolds, 1778–88
Canvas $29\frac{1}{2} \times 24\frac{1}{2}$ in (74.9 × 62.2 cm)

In Malone's estimation Johnson was 'next to Shakespeare'. The two men first met about the time when Johnson was working on his edition of Shakespeare.

A Shakespearean scholar himself, Malone was to become, in Boswell's word, 'Johnsonianissimus', the conscientious collector of Johnsoniana, and the archetype generous scholar to whom everybody turned for advice and assistance. Malone read and commented on the manuscript of Boswell's *Tour to the Hebrides*, and was later to help him to draft, revise, and read the proofs of the *Life of Johnson*. In the darkest moments when Boswell was feeling utterly dejected and depressed, Malone encouraged him to finish his *magnum opus*.

Malone was elected a member of The Club in February 1782, 'an object of ambition to the most eminent men of the day'. He was for many years its treasurer, and was indefatigably clubable in all its affairs.

This portrait was first painted in 1778. About ten years later, Reynolds 'repainted it, making several alterations to the hair, drapery etc.'

National Portrait Gallery, London (NPG 709)

71 · 'THE PLAYS OF WILLIAM SHAKESPEARE, WITH THE CORRECTIONS AND ILLUSTRATIONS OF VARIOUS COMMENTATORS; TO WHICH ARE ADDED NOTES BY SAM. JOHNSON'
Eight volumes
London, J. and R. Tonson and others. 1765
Showing Vol. 1 only at the Preface where Johnson points out the genius of Shakespeare as 'the poet of nature'

Although it was promised in his *Proposals* of 1756 'That the work shall be published on or before Christmas 1757', Johnson's edition of Shakespeare did not appear until October 1765. Whether it was due to the absence of financial pressure, or his reluctance as a perfectionist to let his work go to press until he felt he had achieved his goal, or simply an extended mental and physical breakdown after the anxious *Dictionary* years, or a combination of all these factors, is not known. The long delay had had its critics, not only among his friends and subscribers,

PREFACE.

Shakespeare is above all writers, at least above all modern writers, the poet of nature; the poet that holds up to his readers a faithful mirrour of manners and of life. His characters are not modified by the customs of particular places, unpractised by the rest of the world; by the peculiarities of studies or professions, which can operate but upon small numbers; or by the accidents of transient fashions or temporary opinions: they are the genuine progeny of common humanity, such as the world will always supply, and observation will always find. His persons act and speak by the influence of those general passions and principles by which all minds are agitated, and the whole system of life is continued in motion. In the writings of other poets a character is too often an individual; in those of *Shakespeare* it is commonly a species.

It is from this wide extension of design that so much instruction is derived. It is this which fills the plays of *Shakespeare* with practical axioms and domestick wisdom. It was said of *Euripides*, that every verse was a precept; and it may be said of *Shakespeare*, that from his works may be collected a system of civil and oeconomical prudence. Yet his real power is not shewn in the splendour of particular passages, but by the progress of his fable, and the tenour of his dialogue; and he that tries to recommend him by select quotations, will succeed like

71   [A 3]   the

but also from the caustic pen of the poet Charles Churchill who dubbed him 'Pomposo', the 'insolent and loud, and Vain idol of a scribbling crowd':

> He for *subscribers* baits his hook
> And takes their cash – but where's the book?

Like his *Dictionary*, Johnson's *Shakespeare* became a model for his followers. By including commentaries from his predecessors, by his masterly Preface, and sensible notes, Johnson brought his readers to a closer understanding of Shakespeare as a writer and a poet – all the more important when Shakespeare was frequently altered, adapted, and sentimentalized to suit eighteenth-century taste.

Dr Johnson's House Trust

72 · DAVID GARRICK 1717-79
Thomas Gainsborough (1727-88), 1770
Canvas $29\frac{3}{4} \times 24\frac{7}{8}$ in (75.6 × 63.2 cm)

Unlike Johnson, his former pupil David Garrick, who came with him to London in 1737, quickly made his mark. From his debut in October 1741 as Richard III at Giffard's Theatre to his grand funeral on 1 February 1779 with fifty coaches reaching 'from Charing Cross to the Abbey' ('Madam, there were no more six horses than six phoenixes', Johnson told Burney's wife), his was one long story of triumphs. He was the first of a new breed of theatrical professionals, a manager as well as an actor, who added dignity and art to their work. He rewrote Shakespeare, purchased his own country house, and had a special collection of library and pictures.

But Johnson thought that 'he will disturb us by his buffoonery', and Garrick was not admitted to The Club until 1773.

National Portrait Gallery, London (NPG 5054)

73 · 'JOHNSON AND GARRICK'
[Sir Joshua Reynolds]
London, privately printed, 1816
Inscribed on title:
(1) *To Miss Edgeworth with/Mrs Gwatkins Compts*
(2) *by Gwatkin*
Showing two sides of an argument concerning Garrick. R means Reynolds

Publicly Johnson admitted Garrick's greatness. But in private company he was not prepared to let Garrick's vanity run wild. According to the prefatory note to this little book,

> The following Jeu d'Esprit was written by Sir Joshua Reynolds to illustrate a remark which he had made, 'That Dr Johnson considered Garrick as his property, and would never suffer any one to praise or abuse him but himself.'

This copy was, as the inscription says, given by

73

Reynolds's niece Mrs Theophila Gwatkin to Maria Edgeworth.

Johnson Birthplace Museum (Lichfield City Council)

74 · 'MISCELLANIES IN PROSE AND VERSE'
Anna Williams
London, T. Davies, 1766
Two leaves privately inserted at the front, containing three inscriptions, the first and the last by
Mrs Thrale (afterwards Mrs Piozzi):
> (1) *This Book belongs/to Sir James Fellowes;/ presented to him as the last Testimony of true Regard/ & Esteem by his much/Obliged & faithful Friend/ Hester Lynch Piozzi*
> (2) *The above was/written but a short time before her death which took place at Clifton/on Wednesday night the 2.ᵈ of May 1821 in the 82.ᵈ of her age – JF. –*
> (3) *The Tale of the Fountains was written by Doctor/ Johnson for purpose of filling up this Book: &/he asked H:L:Thrale for something of hers beside ––– She contributed the Three Warnings, &/a Translation of Boileau's Epistle to his Gardener*

Showing part of 'Reflections on a Grave digging in Westminster Abbey' with Mrs Thrale's note in the margin

Throughout his life Johnson was always ready to help his friends and fellow-writers. From prefaces, dedications, essays, poems, to sermons and lectures, the full extent and diversity of his contributions and ghost-writing will probably never be known, owing to his modesty and to the sensitivity of those who requested him originally. Among the numerous publications he assisted is the *Miscellanies of Prose and Verse* by his blind friend and housekeeper. He contributed seven pieces (one doubtful), many of which had previously been printed. Moreover, according to Boswell 'his superior pen' could be detected in four poems by Anna Williams, including 'Reflections on a Grave digging in Westminster Abbey'. Johnson was squeamish about bones. To what extent he had

helped is not clear. He may have helped by adding polishing touches, or, as Mrs Thrale has suggested in the margin of the last stanza, 'These Lines are Johnson's own.'

Johnson Birthplace Museum (Lichfield City Council)

75 · HOLOGRAPH PRAYER WITH CATHERINE CHAMBERS, RECORDED ON 18 OCTOBER 1767
Samuel Johnson

In May 1767, Johnson interrupted his business visit to Oxford and hurried to Lichfield to be near Catherine Chambers, his family servant, who had been gravely ill for some months. He remained there for five months. Having sought the advice from his friend and physician, Thomas Lawrence, and finally known that her case was hopeless, he prayed with her for the last time on Saturday, 17 October. The moving incident is recorded in his diary the following day. It begins;

> Yesterday, October 17 at about ten in the morning I took my leave for ever of my dear old Friend Catherine Chambers, who came to live with my Mother about 1724, and has been but little parted from us since. She buried my Father, my Brother, and my Mother. She is now fifty eight years old.
> I desired all to withdraw, then told her that we were to part for ever, that as Christians we should part with prayer, and [the rest continued as illustrated] swelled eyes and great emotion of tenderness the same hopes. We kissed and parted, I humbly hope, to meet again, and to part no more.

Pembroke College, Oxford

76 · 'DR JOHNSON IN HIS TRAVELLING DRESS'
Thomas Trotter (d. 1803)
Engraving 10⅛ × 7 in (25.7 × 17.8 cm)
Published 18 January 1786, by George Kearsley

Ever since he had read as a boy Martin Martin's *Description of the Western Islands of Scotland* (1703) Johnson had cherished a wish to visit the Hebrides.

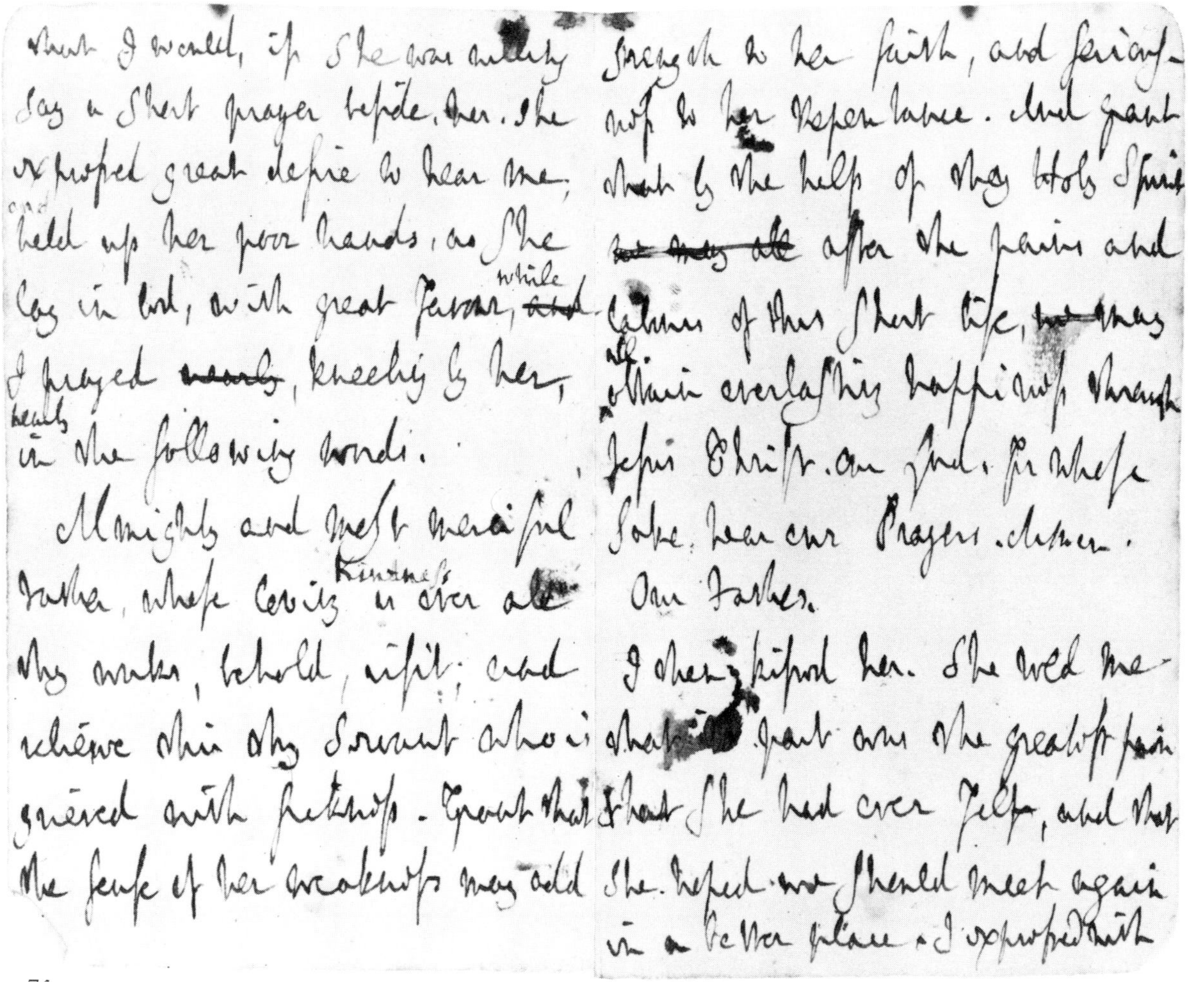
that I would, if She was willing
say a short prayer beside her. She
expressed great desire to hear me,
and held up her poor hands, as She
lay in bed, with great fervour, ~~and~~ while
I prayed ~~nearly~~, kneeling by her, nearly
in the following words.

Almighty and most merciful
Father, whose loving kindness is over all
thy works, behold, visit, and
relieve this thy Servant who is
grieved with sickness. Grant that
the sense of her weakness may add
strength to her faith, and seriousness to her repentance. And grant
that by the help of thy Holy Spirit
~~we may all~~ after the pains and
labours of this short life, ~~we may~~
we all obtain everlasting happiness through
Jesus Christ our Lord, for whose
sake, hear our Prayers. Amen.

Our Father.

I then kissed her. She told me
that to part was the greatest pain
that She had ever felt, and that
She hoped we Should meet again
in a better place. I expressed with

75

On 14 August 1773, he arrived in Edinburgh. Four days later, he set off with Boswell, the obvious guide, on a three months' tour in Scotland, spending nearly two months on the islands.

Boswell writes,

> Upon this tour, when journeying, he wore boots, and a very wide brown cloth great coat, with pockets which might have almost held two large volumes of his folio dictionary; and he carried in his hand a large English oak stick.

The background of this picture is presumably Mull, where on 16 October, Johnson lost his large oak stick.

> It was of great use to him in our wild peregrination; for, ever since his last illness in 1766, he has had a weakness in his knees, and has not been able to walk easily. It had too the properties of a measure; for one nail was driven into it at the length of a foot; another at that of a yard. In return for the services it had done him, he said, this morning he

would make a present of it to some museum; but he little thought he was so soon to lose it. . . . I could not persuade him out of a suspicion that it had been stolen. 'No, no, my friend (said he), it is not to be expected that any man in Mull, who has got it, will part with it. Consider, sir, the value of such a *piece of timber* here!'

Dr JOHNSON *in his Travelling Dress as described in* BOSWELL's *TOUR.*

76

The design of this engraving is probably based on 'a drawing in chalks, from the life', about eighteen months before Johnson died, which was exhibited by Trotter at the Royal Academy in 1785, no. 565.

National Portrait Gallery, London

77 · 'A JOURNEY TO THE WESTERN ISLANDS OF SCOTLAND'

[Samuel Johnson]
London, W. Strahan and T. Cadell, 1775
Showing the uncancelled U4, pp. 295–6

The tour had been the 'pleasantest part of his life', and Johnson had already thought of writing a book about it when he was in the Highlands. When he got back to London by late November 1773, he almost immediately began shaping it in his mind. His speed was such that, despite the two months' break from July to September 1774, when he toured Wales and the Midlands with the Thrales, he was able to see the first issues of the book in print in December.

Johnson's *Journey* was largely an Englishman's first impression of Scotland. With Boswells 'frankness and gaiety' which 'made every body communicative' he was able to find out in detail the living social conditions, the languages, and customs in these parts. He discussed the effect of emigration, and discovered the use of peat. He modesty concluded that 'Novelty and ignorance must always be reciprocal, and I cannot but be conscious that my thoughts on national manners, are the thoughts of one who has seen but little.'

This copy is the one he sent, along with another for George III, to William Hunter (1718–83) on 29 December 1774. It is also interesting in that it contains passages on pages 295 and 296 relating to an account which Johnson has already mentioned on pages 154 and 155. This was subsequently substituted by another passage in later copies of the first edition. Mrs Thrale also received a copy in this very rare, uncancelled, state.

Glasgow University Library (Hunterian Coll. Bo.3.25)

78 · SAMUEL JOHNSON

Sir Joshua Reynolds, *c.* 1775
Canvas, feigned oval, 30 × 24⅞ in (76.2 × 63.2 cm)

[111]

This portrait is usually connected with the following passage in Mrs Piozzi's *Anecdotes of the Late Samuel Johnson, L.LD.* (1786):

> When Sir Joshua Reynolds had painted his portrait looking into the slit of his pen, and holding it almost close to his eye, as was his general custom, he felt displeased, and told me 'he would not be known by posterity for his defects only, let Sir Joshua do his worst.' I said in reply, that Reynolds had no such difficulties about himself, and that he might observe the picture which hung up in the room where we were talking, represented Sir Joshua holding his ear in his hand to catch the sound. 'He may paint himself as deaf if he chuses (replied Johnson); but I will not be *blinking Sam*.'

Northcote in his *Memoirs of Sir Joshua Reynolds* (1813) gives 1775 as the date of the picture, but confuses the issue by referring to Reynolds's self-portrait as 'painted with the ear trumpet'. While Mrs Piozzi was right about Reynolds's self-portrait (painted originally for Streatham Park and now in the Tate Gallery) as 'holding his ear in his hand', she was wrong about Johnson 'looking into the slit

of his pen'. The painting could have been begun earlier if the payment of £36 13s. 1d. (£36.65) from 'Mr Malone' recorded in Reynolds's Ledgers, 12 May 1774, refers to this. Malone was the original owner of the picture.

A personal joke perhaps initially, Reynolds's painting triumphantly transformed his friend's defect into an engaging study. Its vigour and vitality is so akin to Barry's (no. 92) that the possibility that the portrait was finished at a later date cannot be absolutely ruled out. It was engraved by John Hall for the first collected edition of Johnson's *Works* in 1787.

Reynolds's idea seems to have inspired others. A vivid, unfinished, study, attributed to Gilbert Stuart shows an identical pose. Two others painted about the same time, one attributed to Frances Reynolds, and the other to Theophila Palmer (Mrs Gwatkin), although showing Johnson holding a book differently, must also be from the same source. These two look so similar that they could conceivably be by the same hand, which may also be responsible for the engraving by De Claussin, curiously as 'after Northcote', 1813.

Courage Limited

6 · The Thrales and Streatham Park

Professionally and financially Johnson had, to use his own expression, 'seen land'. But the long struggle had exhausted his mental and physical energies. He was 'disturbed with doubts and harassed with vain terrours'. Meeting the Thrales was timely, for when his breakdown came, he was immediately taken to Streatham where, for three months in the summer of 1766, Mrs Thrale nursed him almost single-handedly.

With the Thrales he experienced real family happiness. It was to him in every sense 'one of the great lenitives of life'.

> It is good to wander a little, lest one should dream that all the world was Streatham.

79 · HENRY THRALE 1729?–81
Sir Joshua Reynolds, 1777, for Streatham Park
Canvas 29 × 24½ in (73.7 × 62.2 cm)

Son of a prosperous brewer, Henry Thrale studied at Oxford, succeeded to his father's business in 1758, and was MP for Southwark from 1765 to 1780. He was described by his loyal friend, Arthur Murphy, as having 'the habits of a gentleman; his amiable temper recommended his conversation, and the goodness of his heart made him a sincere friend.'

In 1772, having invested in some foolish adventures, he faced bankruptcy. Although with the help of his wife and Johnson the business recovered, he was never the same 'showy talking man' again.

After Thrale's death, Johnson was one of his executors and helped to manage the brewery before its final sale in May 1781.

Anonymous lender

80 · HESTER LYNCH THRALE 1741–1821 AND HESTER MARIA THRALE 1764–1857
Sir Joshua Reynolds, *c.* 1777, for Streatham Park
Canvas 38½ × 55¼ in (97.8 × 140.3 cm)

'True in *my* portrait above all, there is really no resemblance, and the *character* is less like *my* father's daughter than Pharoah's.' Considered flattering, not like, disguising her shortness, this double portrait was criticized by Mrs Thrale in prose and verse (various versions exist):

> In these features so placid, so cool, so serene,
> What trace of the wit or the Welshwoman's seen?
> What trace of the tender, the rough, the refin'd,
> The soul in which such contrarieties join'd!

In features, however, this portrait is not far from the oil by Robert Edge Pine which shows her in widowhood. Reynolds, in choosing to depict her in this mood of serenity, confirms her fundamental calming influence. When in 1784 she announced her intention to remarry, much to the condemnation of her family and of almost all her friends, Johnson's last reconciliatory words to her were 'to repay for that kindness which soothed twenty years of a life radically wretched'.

Witty, vivacious, learned, and a woman of 'contrarieties', Hester Lynch Salusbury was tutored by her mother. She married Henry Thrale on 11 October 1763, after the sudden death of her father, obedient to the wishes of her mother, but against her own. She soon learned to be a society hostess as well as a woman of business.

Her eldest child Hester Maria, better known through Johnson as Queeney, came under his influence from childhood. She was 'my sweet, dear,

79

80

pretty, little miss', 'my dear charmer', and 'my dearest miss'. To her and to the other Thrale children Johnson showed a most touching concern and kindness towards their education and happiness. Even Queeney's deliberation could be a source of poetical inspiration:

Wear the gown, and wear the hat,
    Snatch thy pleasures while they last,
Hast thou nine lives like a cat,
    Soon those nine lives would be past.

Beaverbrook Art Gallery

[115]

81 ·

81 · STREATHAM PARK, SURREY
Peter Richard Hoare (1772–1849)
Pen and ink and wash 5¼ × 7¼ in (13.3 × 18.4 cm)
Inscribed twice, ink over pencil:
the late Mr Thrale's Streatham

Streatham Park, also known as 'Streatham Place' or later, 'Thrale Place', was Henry Thrale's country home, built by his father. This view represents the house as it was after extensive improvements since 1771. The entire estate, now covering 89 acres, had new wings, walled gardens, sloping lawns, a lake, stables, coachhouses, farm buildings, an icehouse, even a summerhouse for Johnson, in which to meditate and write. Thirteen pictures by Reynolds of the Thrales and their friends were commissioned for

the new library (on the ground floor, extreme right of the house, with bow window).

Peter Richard Hoare was brother-in-law of the seventh child of the Thrales, Sophia (1771–1824) who married Henry Merrik Hoare in August 1807. The drawing was originally in a book of sketches dating from about 1807 to 1840 of places the artist visited, though when he went to Streatham Park is not known. It is possible that he went with his brother and his sister-in-law when the contents of the house were sold in May 1816.

After a fire in 1863 the house was demolished. Johnson's summerhouse, having travelled to Ashgrove in Kent, then back to Streatham Common, is now in the garden at Kenwood, Hampstead.

Mr & Mrs K. K. Yung

82 · ARTHUR MURPHY 1727–1805
Nathaniel Dance (Sir Nathaniel Dance-Holland, 1753–1811), 1777
Canvas 50 × 40 in (127 × 101.6 cm)

Irish journalist, actor, wit, playwright, and lawyer, Murphy met Johnson through a peculiar circumstance. In 1754 he had translated what he thought was an original article from a French journal, but was a *Rambler* essay. His courteous apologies, both in writing and in person, immediately won the warm friendship of Johnson. Knowing that the Thrales wanted to meet more literary friends, Murphy brought Johnson to dinner at their town house at Southwark on 9 January 1765, 'the first time,' as Mrs Thrale writes, 'I ever saw this extraordinary man.' Besides Johnson, Murphy was the only friend remaining loyal and supportive to Mrs Thrale after her second marriage.

This portrait is one of three known versions, and

82

is believed to have been painted for the Thrale daughters. It was engraved by William Ward (1762–1826) in 1805. Their parents already had their portrait of Murphy by Reynolds.

National Portrait Gallery, London (NPG 10)

83 · SAMUEL JOHNSON
Sir Joshua Reynolds, 1772?, for Streatham Park
Canvas 29 × 24⅞ in (70.8 × 63.2 cm)
(*see frontispiece*)

Of all the portraits by Reynolds this is the most difficult to date accurately. The mezzotint by William Doughty (d. 1782), published on 24 June 1779, corresponds with the design of this picture. By then, however, two versions were in progress, if not finished. In Reynolds's Ledgers, two payments are recorded as received from 'Mr Beauclerk' (Topham Beauclerk) for 'a copy of Mr Garrick and Dr Johnson', dated February and November 1779. Beauclerk's version was also of the same design. It was given by Lady Diana Beauclerk to Bennet Langton after her husband's death in 1780. This was first engraved by Thomas Cook in August 1786 and March 1787, and later by James Heath in January 1799.

Johnson's letters to Mrs Thrale telling her on 15 October 1778, 'I have sat twice to Sir Joshua, and he seems to like his own performance. He has projected another in which I am to be busy,' and on 31 October 1778, 'Sir Joshua has finished my picture, it seems to please everybody, but I shall wait to see how it pleases you,' are generally regarded as referring to the Streatham version. While mentioning the portraits at Streatham Park, Mrs Thrale (then as Mrs Piozzi) says in her *Anecdotes of Johnson* (1786) that 'that of Dr Johnson was the last finished'. The *Anecdotes* was written abroad. Her memory was at fault with another portrait of Johnson (no. 78), so she could be inaccurate with this. The last portrait painted for Streatham Park was certainly that of Burney (no. 55), not Johnson. The two letters quoted were first published in her edition of Johnson's *Letters*, 1788. In her copy (no. 89, vol. 2, p. 21), specially inscribed and annotated with great care for her literary executor, Sir James Fellowes (1771–1857), she has put in the margin against the reference to the portrait in the letter of 31 October 1778, 'This was not the Portrait you saw in Streatham Park Library. *That* was painted in 1772.' Johnson, easily the most important member of the Streatham Park circle, could well have been the first sitter when Reynolds began his commission around 1772. The letters then could be referring to Beauclerk's version, and Johnson was asking Mrs Thrale to compare that with Streatham's.

The best known portrait of Johnson, crystalized in Hawkins's description 'there is in it that appearance of a labouring, working mind, of an indolent reposing body, which he had to a very great degree' (Hawkins's edition of Johnson's *Works*, 1787, vol. 11, p. 204), has become ironically the most mysterious. Hawkins, it should be noted, actually had the Langton version in mind, for the sentence immediately before his description reads, 'The picture of him by Sir Joshua Reynolds, which was painted for Mr Beauclerk, and is now Mr Langton's, and scraped in mezzotinto by Doughty, is extremely like'. No portrait of Johnson by Reynolds can be deduced as showing him 'busy', unless of course it means that the 'blinking Sam' portrait (no. 78) was painted around 1778 and not earlier.

The Trustees of the Tate Gallery (887)

84 · 'STREATHAM PARK, SURREY. A CATALOGUE OF THE EXCELLENT AND GENUINE HOUSEHOLD FURNITURE . . . A COLLECTION OF VALUABLE PAINTINGS; . . . ALSO, THE EXTENSIVE AND WELL-SELECTED LIBRARY, AND THE GENUINE PROPERTY OF MRS PIOZZI'
Sold by Auction, by Mr Squibb
Wednesday the 8th of May, 1816, And Four following days (Sunday excepted)

Showing the contents of 'Dr Johnson's Room, Left Wing'

Johnson's room was immediately above the library. Compared with the chaos at Gough Square, or any of his London homes, this was great comfort and luxury.

This sale catalogue is extremely rare. Only three copies are known, of which two are in America.

National Portrait Gallery, London

34

No. 8. *Dr. Johnson's Room, Left Wing.*

LOT
58 A wire fender with brass top, a set of fire-irons, and a hearth rug
59 A 5 feet 9 four-post bedstead, fluted mahogany feet posts, and flowered chintz furniture
60 A wool mattrass, striped case, and a ditto, crankey case
61 Two wool mattrasses, white calico cases
62 Three blankets
63 Three pair of dimity window curtains, with rods, laths, lines and pins
64 A neat japanned 3 feet 6 wash-hand table with two drawers, blue and white basin, ewer, soap cups, and glass decanter
65 A swing glass, 18 by 15, in a mahogany frame
66 A 3 feet 3 commode front dressing chest of four drawers, the top drawer fitted up with rising glass, &c.
67 A walnut-tree bureau, with four drawers under, the top part enclosed by folding glazed doors
68 Five japanned elbow chairs with cane seats, and two stools with matted seats
69 A mahogany bidet with Wedgwood pan, and a ditto night table
70 A deal painted wardrobe with four sliding trays in the upper part, enclosed by folding doors, and three drawers under
71 A Kidderminster carpet as planned to the room
72 A large easy chair with stuffed back and sides, cushion, and cotton cover

Library.

73 A handsome steel cut and pierced fender, and a set of high polished fire irons
74 A fringed hearth rug, 7 feet 6 long

84

85

85 · JOSEPH BARETTI 1719–89

Sir Joshua Reynolds, 1774, for Streatham Park
Canvas 29 × 24½ in (73.7 × 62.2 cm)

A literary image, but an uncomfortable and uneasy character, Reynolds's interpretation seems to agree with practically everybody who knew Baretti. Despite the 'strong powers in his mind', Johnson was aware of his rudeness and violent temper. In 1769 he, Reynolds, and Burke were character witnesses for Baretti at his trial when he was acquitted of murdering a man in a street fight.

Giusseppe Marc Antonio Baretti, from Turin, came to London in 1751, went away in 1760, and finally came to settle in 1766. The success of his *Dictionary of the English and Italian Language* (1760), for which Johnson wrote the Dedication, brought him recognition, and Johnson brought him to Streatham, first as a regular guest, and then from October 1773 as tutor in Italian and Spanish to the children. He was courier to the Thrales' trip with Johnson to France.

According to Baretti, Johnson assured him that after a few years as the children's tutor, 'a rich man like Mr Thrale would make me easy with an annuity for the remainder of my days'. But his incessant quarrels with Mrs Thrale over the ways to discipline the children and other household affairs finally dashed all his hopes of a pension. On 6 July 1776, he walked away to London, 'without uttering a syllable, fully resolved never to see her again'. Twelve years later he revenged her by attacking viciously and publicly her edition of Johnson's *Letters*.

Private Collection

86 · AUTOGRAPH LETTER SIGNED, FROM JOHNSON TO MRS THRALE, 19 JUNE 1775

On a visit to Streatham in the summer of 1775, Boswell brought along his manuscript journal for his tour with Johnson to the Hebrides. He left it behind for those who wished to read it. It might even be a bait to tempt Mrs Thrale to show him her diaries. Johnson read it, and thought it was 'a merry piece'. He later commented, 'One would think the man had been hired to be a spy upon me. He was very diligent, and caught opportunities of writing from time to time.' Mrs Thrale read it too, but being as Boswell put it, his 'rival' for Johnson, she returned the manuscript and offered no comment except that it had 'almost blinded' her. She had thought, like the others, that the journal was Boswell's personal diary only, not realizing that it would in future be used in a book.

Johnson's letters to her during this summer kept mentioning the 'journals'. When she came to publishing his *Letters*, she felt she had to wipe out the references including the paragraph in this letter, dated 19 June 1775, heavily inked out, which reads:

Do you read Boswell's Journals? He moralised, and found my faults, and laid them up to reproach

me. Boswell's narrative is very natural, and therefore very entertaining, he never made any scruple
of showing it to me. He is a very fine fellow. He
has established Rasa's Chieftainship in the Edinburgh
papers, and quieted all commotion in the Hebridean
world. These little things are great to little Man.

And on this she pasted a cutting from another
which reads:

Your dissertation upon Queeny is very deep. I
know not what to say to the chief question. Nature
probably has some part in human characters, and
accident has some part, which has most we will try
to settle when we meet.

*Johnson Birthplace Museum (Lichfield City Council)
(MS 21/12)*

86

87

87 · 'THE GENTLEMAN'S NEW MEMORANDUM
BOOK FOR THE YEAR 1765': DAYS AND MONTHS
CORRESPONDED WITH 1782, AND USED BY
JOHNSON AS A DIARY FOR THAT YEAR
London, J. Dodsley and others
Showing Johnson's diaries for 30 September to
6 October 1782

Henry Thrale died on 4 April 1781. A week later, he
was buried, and with him, Johnson recorded in his
diary, 'many of my hopes and pleasures'. While
Mrs Thrale's attention was romantically drawn to
the Italian musician, Gabriel Piozzi, Johnson realized
that his connections with the old Thrale establish-

SEPTEMBER 1765.   44

EK's ACCOUNT.	Received.			Paid.		
To White				1	1	0
From Strahan	4	4	0			
mark for wages				2	10	0
White				0	5	0
for Dinah				3	9	
from Strahan	20	0	0			
To Francis				2	2	0
To Desmoulins				1	1	0
To White				1	11	6
Strahans				0	10	0
&c						
				5	4	6
in Pocket Gold				13	13	0
Silver				0	16	6
				19	14	0

ment had to come to an end. He paid his last visits to Streatham in September and early October, 1782. Troubled with grief, he turned his mind to study ('we must first pray, and then labour,' as he had written to Mrs Thrale the day after her husband's death). While travelling to and fro, and attending to his usual business, drawing money from Strahan and paying wages, he was also resuming his study of a foreign language. Between 30 September and 5 October he was giving himself 'a little Dutch' lesson every day. On the Sunday he went to the church at Streatham.

Curators of the Bodleian Library, Oxford (MS Don f.6)   88

88 · HOLOGRAPH PRAYER ON LEAVING THE THRALE FAMILY, 6 OCTOBER 1782
Samuel Johnson

Johnson bid the church farewell with a kiss. In his prayer for the day he offered thanks for 'the comforts and conveniences' he had enjoyed with the Thrales, commended all those who had survived to divine protection, and Henry Thrale to divine mercy.

The next morning he was called early, packed his bundles, and read for the last time in the library, selecting passages from St Paul's farewell in the Acts and from the Gospels.

Pembroke College, Oxford

89 · 'LETTERS TO AND FROM THE LATE
SAMUEL JOHNSON, LL.D.'
Hester Lynch Piozzi
Two volumes
London, A. Strahan and T. Cadell, 1788
Inscribed on verso of endpaper:

> *O. B. Fellowes,/grand-son of Sir James Fellowes/to
> whom Mrs Piozzi presented/these Volumes, and for
> whom,/she specially added the copious marginal Notes
> etc./in 1815. – vide p.363./twenty-seven years/after
> the book was/first printed.*

Inscribed on title: *James Butler Fellowes*
Vol. 1 showing pp. 362–3; vol. 2 showing
title-page

Published almost four years after the death of Johnson,
Mrs Piozzi's had remained for over a century until
G. B. Hill's edition in 1892, the only substantial and
authoritative edition of his letters. It diverted the
attention of those who condemned her second marriage. It helped to whet the appetite of Johnsonian
scholars and enthusiasts in general. Malone, for

example, sat up all night and only managed to finish
the first volume. He thought the book was 'in general very pleasing, and exactly what I had expected'.
Most important of all, it revealed the informal
Johnson, Johnson 'in his undress, that is, the undress
of his mind, which, unlike that of the body, was
never slovenly'. The intimate and enjoyable relationship he had with the Thrales, his daily life and
travels while he was away from them, including the
long letters he wrote from Scotland, were all made
public for the first time.

Reflecting on her earlier years in 1815, Mrs Piozzi
was touched with sadness. She had followed Johnson's
advice and filled her diaries, her 'Thraliana'. Between
1775 and 1776 she had lost three of her children,
including her only son, aged ten. With the fiery
Baretti around, Johnson not always amiable, and
her husband not always there when needed, she had
had, as she writes in the margin on page 363, her
'afflictions'.

*Johnson Birthplace Museum (Lichfield City Council)
(Hay Hunter Collection)*

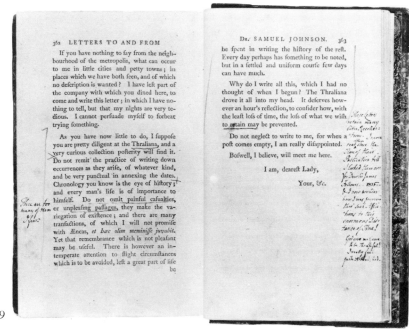

89

7 · Last years

In his last eight years, Johnson's fertile mind remained actively engaged. His critical judgement was exemplified fully by his last major work, now commonly known as *The Lives of the English Poets*, of the seventeenth and eighteenth centuries. He began his literary life as a poet, and he died a champion of the poet's cause.

90 · 'POLITICAL TRACTS. CONTAINING, THE FALSE ALARM. FALKLAND'S ISLANDS. THE PATRIOT; AND, TAXATION NO TYRANNY'
[Samuel Johnson]
London, W. Strahan and T. Cadell, 1776
Inscribed:
(1) by Johnson *To the reverend/Dr Wetherel/ Master of University College*
(2) by unknown hand, presumably Nathan Wetherell (1726–1807) *The handwriting of the celebrated/learned and good D.ʳ Johnson*
Showing title-page

Ever since becoming a hack journalist for *The Gentleman's Magazine* Johnson had been producing treatises and reviews on political subjects. In later years he actively helped Henry Thrale in his election campaigns. And William Strahan, MP since 1774, even suggested that he might enter parliament.

In his last four political pamphlets, written between 1770 and 1775 and originally published separately, Johnson not only shows a firm grasp of the complexities of the current issues – Wilkes's expulsion by Parliament, the Falkland Islands crisis, true patriotism, and the question of taxing American colonies – but also expresses his underlying principles as a lover of peace and order. As a citizen of his country, he respects authority. 'All government supposes subjects, all authority implies obedience.' He condemns 'epidemic patriotism'. 'He is no lover of his country that unnecessarily disturbs its peace.'

> But as peace is the end of war, it is the end likewise of preparations for war; and he may be justly hunted down as the enemy of mankind, that can chuse to snatch by violence and bloodshed, what gentler means can equally obtain.

Johnson Birthplace Museum (Lichfield City Council) (Hay Hunter Collection)

91 · SAMUEL JOHNSON
Joseph Nollekens (1737–1823), 1777
Lead cast of bust 20½ in (52.1 cm) high
Inscribed on mahogany base: RAMBLER

Johnson knew and like the sculptor's family, but hated the sittings,

> which rather vexed the artist, who, upon opening the street-door, a vulgarity he was addicted to, peevishly whined – 'Now, Doctor, you *did* say you would give my busto half an hour before dinner, and the dinner has been waiting this long time.' To which the Doctor's reply was, 'Bow-wow-wow'.

A good likeness, the bust was nevertheless condemned by Mrs Thrale, Frances Reynolds, Mrs David Garrick, and Lucy Porter. The objection was really the hair. For while trying to make the sitter 'more like an ancient poet', Nollekens had borrowed 'the flowing locks of a sturdy Irish beggar'.

Very few original plaster casts are extant. This cast is of very fine quality and, being in lead, is also unique, since no other lead casts of Nollekens's works are known to exist.

91

92

No marble version is known to have been executed by Nollekens, but at least three copies are extant. The first is by John Bacon, and was bequeathed by Samuel Whitbread to Pembroke College, Oxford, in 1796. The second, belonging to the National Portrait Gallery, is by E. Hodges Baily and is dated 1828. The third, wrongly assigned to Nollekens and probably dates around 1830 is in Westminster Abbey. A terracotta, by A. L. Vago, is at the Athenaeum.

Victoria & Albert Museum, London (A63 & A – 1926)

92 · SAMUEL JOHNSON
James Barry (1741–1806), 1778–80
Canvas, oval $23\frac{7}{8} \times 20\frac{7}{8}$ in (60.6 × 53 cm)

This vivid study must arguably be from life even though no sittings are recorded. Johnson knew Barry at the time when this was made, and later supported him as a member of the short-lived Essex-Head Club in 1783.

The sketch is a study for Barry's fifth and last but one mural, 'The Distribution of Premiums', for his epic series *The Progress of Human Culture*, now in the

Society of Arts. In the mural, Johnson appears between the beautiful Duchesses of Rutland and Devonshire. In this study, reduced from a rectangular, the painted out figure next to him is believed to be Mrs Elizabeth Montagu who did have a masculine profile.

An etching by Anker Smith was published on 1 March 1808.

National Portrait Gallery, London (NPG 1185)

93 · 'MEMOIRS OF THE LIFE OF DAVID GARRICK'
Thomas Davies
A New Edition [Second]
Two volumes
London, 1780
Inscribed:
> *To His honour'd Friend and/Patron*
> *Dr. Samuel Johnson/from the Authour*

Vol. 1 showing page 1 of the text; vol. 2 showing title-page

The first paragraph:
> All excellence has a right to be recorded. I shall therefore think it superfluous to apologize for writing the life of a man who, by an uncommon assemblage of private virtues, adorned the highest eminence in a public profession.

is by Johnson and, according to the Preface by Davies, the book was 'prompted and encouraged' by Johnson, who had also supplied the early part of 'Mr Garrick's life'.

Davies probably addressed Johnson as 'Friend and Patron' deliberately. For over the years, after he had quitted his stage career, he had on many occasions received kindness and assistance from Johnson. His bookselling business was frequently in difficulty. Johnson had lent him money, asked others to contribute, encouraged him to write, and even forgiven him for publishing without permission or consultation in 1773 the first collected edition of Johnson's works, some of which were spurious.

Johnson Birthplace Museum (Lichfield City Council)

94 · JOHNSON'S NOTES FOR 'LIFE OF POPE'
Bound in a volume of *Johnsoniana*, London,
John Murray, 1836
Showing page 1, entitled 'Poetry Study'. On the opposite page is attached the title-page of Clement Marot's *Opera*, 1573, a book owned by Johnson in 1732

In a characteristic understatement Johnson informed Boswell, on 3 May 1777, of his final major literary project. 'I am engaged to write little Lives, and little Prefaces, to a little edition of the English Poets.' Biographies and the minds and workings of poets had been his chief interest, and he set about his task almost immediately. Because of his immense admiration for Alexander Pope, his professionalism, and his superb craftsmanship, Johnson savoured him to the last. By September 1780 he found his progress was slow, and he blamed it on his indolence. 'I have not at all studied; nor written diligently. I have Swift and Pope yet to write, Swift is just begun', he noted in his diary on his birthday.

His *Life of Pope* is the longest in the series: in one volume, occupying 373 pages. To organize his material and to help him to plan his essay he made notes. Two sets of these are extant, one containing twenty-three leaves, which originally belonged to George Steevens (1736–1800), is in the British Library; the other, containing five leaves, which originally belonged to Boswell, is now shown. The first was partially extracted and quoted at random by Isaac D'Israeli in his *Curiosities of Literature* (1834, Vol. IV, pp. 180–4, and later editions) and was later analysed in F. W. Hilles's fascinating account of 'The Making of the Life of Pope' (in *New Light on Dr Johnson*, New Haven, 1959). Professor Hilles did not, however, refer to the second set.

Neither set is dated, nor does it necessarily follow that since one is longer than the other, the shorter should be earlier. The notes now shown on 'Poetry Study' relate to the second part in the *Life of Pope* which deals with his character, his method, and his status as a poet. The corresponding page in the

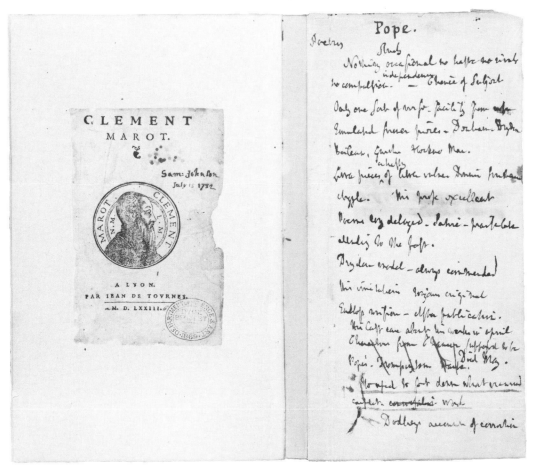

94

British Library set is substantially the same, and the first few lines read:

> Nothing occasional. no haste no
> rivals. no compulsion.
> Practised only one form of verse
> facility from use
> Emulated former pieces. Coopers
> hill. Dryden's Ode.
> &c

The sets of notes are not an outline for the essay. They are in order only to a certain extent. Johnson's analysis of Denham's *Cooper's Hill* and Dryden's *Mac Flecknoe*, for example, are in the third section of the *Life*. Sometimes, as if to remind himself of the vital points and try them out, he repeats them on another page as, on the second leaf of the Victoria & Albert Museum set, he has written

> His poem never occasional
> Long delayed – Satire and praise late
> Confined to one mode more than any other
> writer. Facility by habit
> &c

The notes, therefore, are more like Johnson's mental gems rained on to his blank pages.

Victoria & Albert Museum, London (Dyce 5316)

108

Of genius, that power which constitutes a Poet, that quality without which judgement is cold, and knowledge is inert, that energy which collects, combines, amplifies, and animates, the superiority must, with some hesitation, be allowed to Dryden. It is not to be inferred that of this poetical vigour Pope had only a little, because Dryden had more, for every other writer since Milton, must give place to Pope, and even of Dryden it must be said that he has brighter paragraphs, he has not better poems. Dryden's performances were always hasty, either excited by some external occasion, or extorted by domestick necessity. he composed with little consideration, and published with little correction. When his mind could supply, at call, or gather in one excursion, was all that he sought, and all that he gave. The dilatory caution of Pope enabled him to condense his sentiments, to multiply his images, and to accumulate whatever study might produce, or chance might supply. The flights of Dryden therefore are higher, but Pope continues longer on the wing. Of Dryden's fire the blaze is brighter, of Pope's the heat is regular and constant. Dryden often surpasses expectation, and Pope never falls below it. Dryden is read with frequent astonishment, and Pope with perpetual delight.

95

95 · A PAGE FROM THE MANUSCRIPT OF THE
'LIFE OF POPE'
Samuel Johnson

Having explained Pope's method of composition,
his choice of form and subject, and how he modelled
on Dryden, Johnson proceeds to compare the two
poets. He now reaches the climax where, by com-
paring the geniuses of Pope and Dryden, he gives
his definition of genius.

As Percy writes, Johnson worked from memory,
he 'never composed what we call a foul draft on
paper of anything he published, but used to revolve
the subject in his mind, and turn and form every
period, till he had brought the whole to the highest
correctness, and the most perfect arrangement'. From
his little notes, Johnson produced his masterpiece.
The manuscript of the *Life of Pope* is the longest
extant of Johnson's prose works. Of the 184 pages,
only 20 are not in his handwriting, and these are
transcripts by Mrs Thrale and George Steevens of
Pope's works and letters.

For his passage on genius, Johnson needed no
notes. The tidy manuscript, judging by the handwriting and the even density of the ink, appears to
have been written in one breath. In its printed form,
only a few words have been altered: on line seven,
he has reinstated 'he has' for 'but'; and on line
fourteen, he has printed 'If the flights' instead of
'The flights', and he has omitted 'but'.

The Pierpont Morgan Library, New York (MA 205)

96 · 'PREFACES, BIOGRAPHICAL AND CRITICAL,
TO THE WORKS OF THE ENGLISH POETS'
Samuel Johnson
Sixty-eight volumes
London, by J. Nichols for C. Bathurst and others,
1779–81
Bookplate of: *Francis Mills*
Showing title-page of Vol. 1 of *Prefaces* (no. 59 of
this set); and pp. 260–1 of Vol. 7, *Life of Pope*
(no. 65 of this set)

260   P O P E.

Of composition there are different
methods. Some employ at once memory and invention, and, with little in-
termediate use of the pen, form and
polish large masses by continued meditation, and write their productions only
when, in their own opinion, they have
completed them. It is related of Virgil, that his custom was to pour out a
great number of verses in the morning,
and pass the day in retrenching exube-
rances and correcting inaccuracies. The
method of Pope, as may be collected
from his translation, was to write his
first thoughts in his first words, and
gradually to amplify, decorate, rectify,
and refine them.

With

96

P O P E.   261

With such faculties, and such disposi-
tions, he excelled every other writer in
poetical prudence; he wrote in such a
manner as might expose him to few
hazards. He used almost always the
same fabrick of verse; and, indeed, by
those few essays which he made of any
other, he did not enlarge his reputation.
Of this uniformity the certain consequence was readiness and dexterity. By
perpetual practice, language had in his
mind a systematical arrangement; having
always the same use for words, he had
words so selected and combined as to
be ready at his call. This increase of
facility he confessed himself to have
perceived in the progress of his translation.

R 3   But

'Only one sort of verse – facility from use' in no. 94 forms the basis of the paragraph on p. 261 in his *Life of Pope*.

Johnson's *Prefaces* were published in two instalments: the first four volumes came out in 1779, and the last six in 1781. For these lucid, balanced, and highly readable *Lives*, pioneering works of biographical and literary criticism, Johnson received from his publishers a total sum of £415. Considering his literary status at the time, he could have asked for that for the *Life of Pope* alone. The genius was a 'blockhead' after all. He saw no reason to complain, 'not that they have paid me too little, but that I have written too much.'

Sir William Rees-Mogg

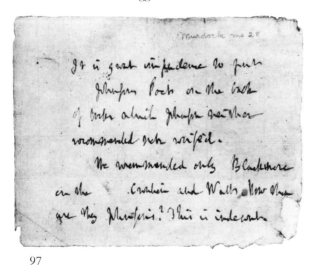

97

97 · HOLOGRAPH NOTE ON THE IMPROPRIETY OF THE TITLE 'JOHNSON'S POETS'
Samuel Johnson

The choice of the poets came from the publishers. In addition to their list of forty-seven Johnson suggested five: Sir Richard Blackmore, Isaac Watts, John Pomfret, Thomas Yalden, and James Thomson. Simultaneously printed with his *Prefaces* (or *Lives*) were selections of the works of the poets in fifty-six volumes, in which Johnson practically had no part. When the sets were ready, with or without the poems, many of them were labelled 'Johnson's Poets' on their backs. This did not conform to his idea of truth. It was 'great impudence' and 'indecent', he writes, since he 'neither recommended nor revised'.

*Houghton Library, Harvard University
(Murdock MS28)*

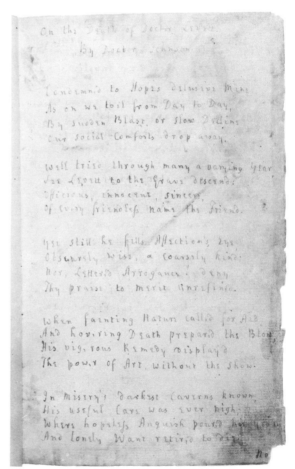

98

98 · TRANSCRIPT OF JOHNSON'S 'ON THE DEATH OF DOCTOR LEVETT'
Elizabeth Carter

Robert Levet (or Levett, 1705–82) died on 17 January 1782. He had been Johnson's inmate and friend for over thirty years. No one outside or inside his household had anything complimentary to say about this obscure physician who walked for miles to treat the poor. Johnson alone remembered affectionately his missions and his virtues.

This transcript by Johnson's friend, Elizabeth Carter, was originally attached to her copy of *A Journey to the Western Islands of Scotland, 1775.*

Anonymous lender

99 · SAMUEL JOHNSON
John Opie (1761–1807), 1783–4
Canvas, 30¼ × 25 in (76.8 × 63.5 cm)

Two identical versions of this portrait are known: this one formerly belonged to Sir John St Aubyn (1758–1839); and the other, which originally belonged to George Horne (1730–92), Bishop of Norwich, whom Johnson knew, is now in the Houghton Library, Harvard University. Both are sensitively and thinly painted, with the Harvard version slightly impasted on the wig.

The date of the first sitting for the portrait is given in a letter from Johnson to Mrs Thrale, 19 June 1783, 'On Monday the 16 I sat for my picture, and walked a considerable way with little inconvenience.' Although the artist is not named, there is little doubt that Opie was meant. For in the same afternoon, Johnson suffered a paralytic stroke which deprived him of his speech for a few days. Gradually he recovered, and by 10 July he was well enough to visit Bennet Langton at Rochester in Kent. This suggestion of Opie is supported by a letter from the Rev. Michael Lort (1725–90) to his friend Thomas Percy, dated 7 August 1783,

> Dr Johnson is recovered, and gone to Mr Langton's at Rochester. Before he went he sat to Opie, the famous self-taught Cornish painter, for his picture, and who I am told has given a just but not flattering likeness.

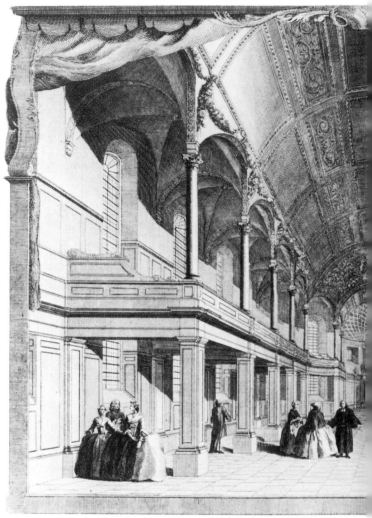

100

In the following spring, after his race up the stairs at the Royal Academy on 24 April, Johnson resumed sitting for Opie, though for which version it is not known.

A mezzotint by Charles Townley was published in Berlin in 1786.

Private Collection

[132]

100 · ST CLEMENT DANES, IN THE STRAND
John Boydell (1719–1804) after Thomas Boydell
Engraving 11¾ × 17 in (29.8 × 43.2 cm)
Published by John Boydell, 1751

Johnson began the New Year of 1784 with a customary prayer asking for the removal of 'scruples' and
'perplexities' from his mind, little suspecting that ill
health which had been troubling him since December
was to lead to a heart attack. This in turn led to a
long confinement to his house. On 21 April, he
wrote to Mrs Thrale,

> After a confinement of one hundred twenty nine
> days, more than the third part of a year, and no
> inconsiderable part of human life, I this day re-
> turned thanks to God in St Clement's Church, for
> my recovery, a recovery in my seventy fifth year
> from a distemper which few in the vigour of youth
> are known to surmount.

Museum of London (49.34/34)

101 · LUNARDI'S ASCENT FROM THE ARTILLERY
GROUND MOORFIELDS, SEPT. 15TH 1784
John James Brewer (fl. 1779/80), 1784
Hand-coloured etching, 14¾ × 20¼ in
(37.5 × 51.4 cm)

The 'Mr Sober' who found daily amusement in
chemistry, who first greeted his friend Arthur
Murphy 'covered with soot, like a chimney-sweeper,
in a little room, as if he had been acting Lungs in the
Alchemist, making aether', and whose 'furnace' at
Streatham Park nearly ruined all Henry Thrale's
lavish work on the mansion, found a new interest
in the current craze over balloon ascents. Johnson
understood the principle perfectly, as can be seen in
his letter to Mrs Thrale of 22 September 1783:

> The chymical philosophers have discovered a body
> (which I have forgotten, but will enquire), which,
> dissolved by an acid, emits a vapour lighter than
> the atmospherical air. This vapour is caught, among
> other means, by tying a bladder, compressed upon
> the bottle in which the dissolution is performed;
> the vapour rising swells the bladder, and fills it.
> The bladder is then tied and removed, and another
> applied, till as much of this light air is collected as is
> wanted. Then a large spherical case is made, and
> very large it must be, of the lightest matter that can
> be found, secured by some method, like that of
> oiling silk, against all passage of air. Into this are
> emptied all the bladders of light air, and if there is

[133]

101

light air enough it mounts into the clouds, upon the same principle as a bottle filled with water will sink in water, but a bottle filled with aether would float. It rises till it comes to air of equal tenuity with its own, if wind or water does not spoil on the way. Such, Madam, is an air ballon.

His interest kept his friends enquiring. By the time Lunardi had made his ascent, Johnson had had more than enough. He told Reynolds 'Do not write about the ballon, whatever else You may think Proper to say.' He did not witness the occasion. Instead, he wondered about the next stage: how can a balloon be guided. Or, he 'had rather now find a medicine that can ease an asthma'.

The Trustees of the British Museum (1899–4–20–103)

102 · HOLOGRAPH TRANSLATION OF HORACE, 'ODES', BOOK IV, vii
Samuel Johnson

Dated 'November 1784' overleaf. If Boswell's suggestion 'in the country' is right, this could only have been written during his last visit to the Midlands, either at Lichfield or on his return journey to London.

It was a long and exceptionally cold winter in 1784. Snow fell in October. The poet mused over the momentary thaw, and the changing seasons. In his last English poem, Johnson returned to his teenage favourite, Horace:

The snow dissolv'd no more is seen,
The fields, and woods, behold, are green,

The changing year renews the plain
The rivers know their banks again . . .

All this, however,

Proclaims mortality to Man.

Anonymous lender

The snow dissolv'd no more is seen
The fields, and woods, ~~again~~ ʰᵉˡᵈ are green,
The changing year renews the plain
The rivers know their banks again
The sprightly Nymph and naked grace
The ᵐᵃᶻʸ ~~mingled~~ dance together trace . .
The changing year's succession plain
Proclaims mortality to Man.
Rough Winter's blasts to Spring give way
Spring yield to Summer's sovereign ray
Then Summer sinks in autumn's reign
And Winter chills the world again
Her losses soon the Moon supplies
But wretched Man, when once he lies
Where Priam and his Sons are laid
Is nought than ashes and a shade

102

103

103 · SAMUEL JOHNSON
Unknown artist, *c.* 1784
Canvas 30 × 25 in (76.2 × 63.5 cm)

For almost a century this portrait had been known as Reynolds's last portrait of Johnson, painted for his friend John Taylor (1711–88). It was first listed in Graves and Cronin's *A History of the Works of Sir Joshua Reynolds* (1899–1901, vol. 2, p. 521). Its owner then was A. E. Watts Russell who sold it at Christie's, 20 June 1919, lot 82. The famous American collector, A. Edward Newton subsequently bought it in August 1922, from John McFadden of Philadelphia who had been its owner since 1920. McFadden either bought it from Agnews, or via Agnews from the sale. An Agnews label is attached to the back of the frame.

Graves and Cronin, as Sir Ellis Waterhouse has warned, 'should be used with great caution'.

No payments from John Taylor are recorded in Reynolds's Ledgers. On stylistic ground it is difficult to reconcile this portrait with Reynolds's works of the late 1770s or early 1780s. The paint thinly applied, the modelling of the head in particular, cannot compare with, for example, the portraits of Burney (no. 55) or Strahan (nos. 38).

As a portrait of Johnson it is much more reliable. In features, it corresponds especially with Barry's painting (no. 92) and the death-mask bust (no. 105). That Johnson is not wearing his usual bushy wig needs not be worrying. As Laetitia Hawkins writes, 'His wig in common was cut and bushy, if by chance he had one that had been dressed in separate curls, it gave him a disagreeable look, not suited to his years or character.' Johnson is seen in a wig 'dressed in separate curls' in another portrait: a

drawing by James Roberts dated 'Oxon 1784' (on loan from a private collection to Pembroke College, Oxford). This could possibly be conceived as a study for a painting, showing Johnson looking more to the left, and with his fingers interlaced. It shows a similarly long face, long eyebrows, and pouting lower lip. But Roberts's oil paintings are very scarce. While his portrait of Hawkins (no. 16) has a similar coarseness, it differs considerably in colouring.

James P. Magill Library, Haverford College, Haverford

104 · 'PRAYERS AND MEDITATIONS, COMPOSED BY SAMUEL JOHNSON, LLD'
Published from his manuscripts, by George Strahan
London, T. Cadell, 1785
Showing Johnson's last prayer, 5 December 1784

216   PRAYERS AND

[The following Prayer was compofed and ufed by Doctor Johnfon previous to his receiving the Sacrament of the Lord's Supper, on Sunday December 5, 1784.]

ALmighty and moft merciful Father, I am now, as to human eyes it feems, about to commemorate, for the * laft time, the death of thy Son Jefus Chrift our Saviour and Redeemer. Grant, O Lord, that my whole hope and confidence may be in his merits, and thy mercy; enforce and accept my imperfect repentance; make this commemoration available to the confirmation of my faith, the eftablifhment of my hope, and the enlargement of my cha-

* [He died the 13th following.]

rity;

MEDITATIONS.   217

rity; and make the death of thy Son Jefus Chrift effectual to my redemption. Have mercy upon me, and pardon the multitude of my offences. Blefs my friends; have mercy upon all men. Support me, by thy Holy Spirit, in the days of weaknefs, and at the hour of death; and receive me, at my death, to everlafting happinefs, for the fake of Jefus Chrift. Amen.

104

On 16 November 1784 Johnson was back in London. His condition worsening, he realized his end was near. On 5 December he asked George Strahan (1744–1824), vicar of Islington and second son of his printer friend, William, to conduct the last communion. Hawkins, who was present, noticed that,

> Previous to reading the exhortation, Johnson knelt, and with a degree of fervour that I had never been witness to before, uttered the following most eloquent and energetic prayer.

In printing this last prayer of Johnson, Strahan left out the clause 'forgive and accept my late conversion' which comes before 'enforce and accept my imperfect repentance', to avoid misinterpretation, not realizing that one of the definitions in his *Dictionary* for 'conversion' is 'Change from rebrobation [sic] to grace, from a bad to a holy life.'

Sir William Rees-Mogg

105 · SAMUEL JOHNSON
William Cumberland Cruikshank (1745–1800) and James Hoskins (d. 1791), 1784
Plaster cast of bust incorporating death-mask, $24\frac{1}{2}$ in (62.2 cm) high

In his *Biographical Sketch of Dr Samuel Johnson*, London, 1785, Thomas Tyers wrote, 'His face and shoulders were moulded and taken off since his death, (alas! how changed from him!) by Hoskins, of St. Martin's-lane, from which a bust is made.' But according to a letter (in NPG archive) written probably in 1878 from Isabella Hutchins to her brother, the cast was taken, 'under the direction' of her grandfather, William Cumberland Cruikshank, the anatomist and one of the physicians attending Johnson on his last days. These two conflicting accounts can perhaps be explained that whereas Cruikshank supervized the casting of the mask, the whole bust, made in three sections – the mask, ears, and body – was the responsibility of Hoskins.

National Portrait Gallery, London (NPG 4685)

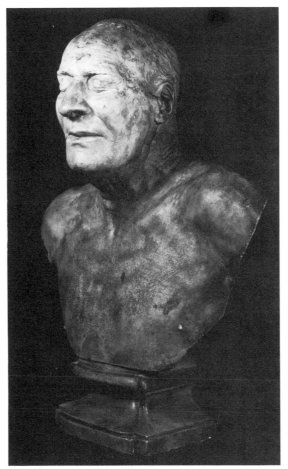

105

106 · PROBATE COPY OF JOHNSON'S WILL
Will dated 8 December, Codicil 9 December, and proved 18 December 1784

As a lawyer and one of Johnson's executors, Hawkins had the unrewarding task of preparing his will. Their first discussion in February ended in disagreement, for Hawkins thought his idea of leaving his servant, Frank Barber, an annuity of £70, too generous. Using Hawkins's draft, Johnson finally dictated to George Strahan on 8 December his will, and on the following day, the codicil. The contents were public knowledge after Johnson's funeral on 20 December. *The London Chronicle*, for example, printed the full details in the issue of 23 – 25 December.

A number of Johnson's books were bequeathed to those who were near him at the time of his death. Hawkins, for example, received his Holinshed's and Stowe's *Chronicles* and other books; Bennet Langton, his great Polyglot Bible; and Reynolds, his 4th edition of the *Dictionary*. In monetary terms, the credit held by his friends, Langton, Percy, and Barclay and Perkins (successors to Thrale's brewery), the cash he left, together with the 3 per cent annuities in 'the public funds', came to just over £2300. According to Hawkins, his Birthplace fetched £235 in an auction in 1785. The bulk of his estate, which included the sale of his library, after deduction from settling debts, expenses, and legacies, went to Frank Barber and his family. This came to a sum 'a little short of £1500'. Johnson was, to use his own expression, 'nobilissimus'.

Dr Johnson's House Trust

107 · SILVER TEAPOT
Hallmark: Edward Wakelin (d. 1784) and
John Parker, *c.* 1758–77
Height 4 in (12.1 cm)
Engraved:

> *We are told by Lucian, that the earthen lamp, which had administered to the Lucubrations of Epictetus, was at his Death purchased for the enormous sum of 3000 Drachmas: why then? may not Imagination equally amplify the Value of this unadorned Vessel, long employed for the Infusion of that favourite Herb, whose enlivening Virtues are said to have so often protracted the elegant & edifying Lucubrations of SAMUEL JOHNSON; the zealous Advocate of that innocent Beverage, against its declared Enemy Jonas Hanway. It was weighed out for sale, under the Inspection of Sr J.^{no} Hawkins, at the very Minute when they were in the next Room closing the Incision, through which Mr Cruikshank had explored the ruinated*

107

> *Machinery of its dead Master's Thorax – so Bray (the Silversmith conveyed there in Sr Johns Carriage thus hastily to buy the Plate) informed its present Possessor HENRY CONSTANTINE NOWELL by whom it was for its celebrated Services, on the 1.st of Novr 1788 rescued from the undiscriminating Obliterations of the Furnace.*

This teapot is probably the one Johnson referred to in his diary on 28 April 1771 when he took stock of his possessions. Under 'Plate' he noted that he had a teapot worth £7 and a coffee pot worth £10. Johnson was, as he describes himself in his review of Jonas Hanway's *A Journal of Eight Days Journey from Portsmouth to Kingston upon Thames, &c. With An Essay on Tea* (1756),

> a hardened and shameless Tea-drinker, who has for twenty years diluted his meals with only the infusion of this fascinating plant, whose kettle has scarcely time to cool, who with Tea amuses the evening, with Tea solaces the midnight, and with Tea welcomes the morning.

Henry Constantine Nowell, the first proud owner of this relic, was better known as Henry Constantine Jennings (1731–1819), or 'Dog' Jennings, the eccentric collector, who purchased from Rome at a bargain price a marble dog thought to be worth 'a thousand guineas'.

Anonymous lender

108 · 'A CATALOGUE OF THE VALUABLE LIBRARY OF BOOKS, OF THE LATE LEARNED SAMUEL JOHNSON'
Christie's, 16 February 1785, and
three following days
Inscribed: *Phillips MS/25852*
Showing the last page, with price list opposite

The least forgivable act of Hawkins is perhaps his handling of the sale of Johnson's library. A scholar, collector, and a generous benefactor to the British Museum, Hawkins should have appreciated the full significance of his friend's collection: the working library of an extraordinary professional writer, the 'Great Cham of Literature'.

Perhaps the thought of the money going to Frank Barber did not inspire him, and he acted hastily. Having discovered the experienced auctioneer, Samuel Paterson, away abroad, Hawkins decided not to wait and handed over the business to James Christie whose firm produced an inaccurate, incomplete, and frequently incomprehensible catalogue.

Recent painstaking and illuminating researches have succeeded in unravelling the mysteries of the 650 lots (of books) and the 12 lots (of prints), which amount to nearly 3000 volumes and over 146 prints. The diversity and magnitude of Johnson's readings are now much better known. Besides the expected categories of literature, classics, religion, and philosophy, there are many of foreign languages, medicine, natural history, science, law, topography, politics, economics, sociology, education, and others. Some, like lots 644 and 649, are now found to be in Yale University Library and the British Library. But many unspecified items, such as lot 635, will remain a mystery.

Although copies of this catalogue are not rare, this is one of two known copies with complete list of prices and purchasers.

Houghton Library, Harvard University

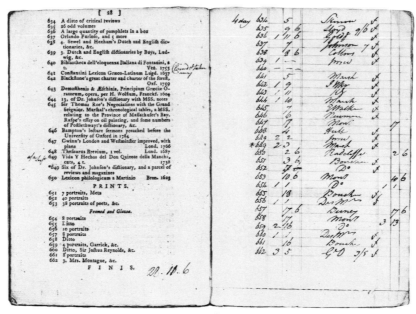

108

8 · Early biographies

A selection of six of the many lives and memoirs of Johnson which appeared after his death is shown in this section. Five of the authors were personally known to him. They vary in length, approach, as well as interpretation.

109 · 'THE LIFE OF SAMUEL JOHNSON, LLD'
[William Cooke]
The Second Edition
London, G. Kearsley, 1785
Inscribed: *R. Smith-Dampier/September 1926*
Bookplate of: *Lt. Col. F:R:C:Grant*
Showing frontispiece and title-page

Published on 27 December 1784, a fortnight after Johnson's death, this helped to satisfy the immediate curiosity. The *Life* is generally a chronological account, without any attempt at being critical. Iconographically, however, it provides a realistic portrait, an etching dated 15 February 1782 and made from life, by Thomas Trotter, which, as in the death-mask bust, shows the scrofula scars Johnson had since childhood. Originally intended as a frontispiece to the second volume of *The Beauties of Johnson*, first published by G. Kearsley in 1782, it was considered 'very ugly' and therefore suppressed. The Wedgwood medallion was based on this.

Dr Johnson's House Trust

110 · 'MEMOIRS OF THE LIFE AND WRITINGS OF THE LATE DR SAMUEL JOHNSON'
[William Shaw]
London, J. Walker, 1785
Showing pp. 110–111, Johnson's relationship with his wife

Shaw knew Johnson. He was able to solicit the help of his friends Thomas Davies, James Elphinston, and his servant, Mrs Desmoulins. From Mrs Desmoulins he constructed his account of the problems between Johnson and his wife, which Boswell later tried to gloss over. Its critical approach must owe its inspiration to Johnson himself.

Curators of the Bodleian Library, Oxford (210 m. 215)

109

111 · 'ANECDOTES OF THE LATE SAMUEL JOHNSON, LLD, DURING THE LAST TWENTY YEARS OF HIS LIFE'
Hester Lynch Piozzi
London, T. Cadell, 1786

Inscribed:

(1) *O. B. Fellowes*
(2) *This copy of the Anecdotes was/found at Bath – covered with dirt – the/book having been long out of Print – &/after being bound & was presented to me/by my excellent Friend H.L.P. – – – J.F.*
(3) by Mrs Piozzi *This little dirty Book is/kindly accepted by/Sir James Fellowes/from his Obliged Friend/H.L.Piozzi/14:Feb:/1816*
(4) *Given to my dear/daughter Beatrice by/her loving Father/J.B.F. 1898*

Showing pp. 296–7, description of Johnson in verse and prose. The verse was written for the portrait by Reynolds (no. 83)

The 1000 copies were all sold out on the first day the book came out on 25 March 1786. An intimate friend, a much cherished pupil, Mrs Piozzi was able to present a casual yet human account; anecdotal as it promises, but shrewd and entertaining. But writing it abroad, she had only her 'Thraliana' to draw on. Her critics, Boswell obviously included, did not hesitate to point out her inaccuracies and inconsistencies.

Johnson Birthplace Museum (Lichfield City Council) (Hay Hunter Collection)

112 · 'THE LIFE OF SAMUEL JOHNSON, LLD'
Sir John Hawkins
London, J. Buckland and others, 1787
Monogram: *JWH*
Bookplate of: *John Walker Heneage*
Showing pp. 250–1, Johnson and the Ivy-Lane Club

Elizabeth Carter summed up this official biography appropriately, 'His character of Dr Johnson is impartially, and very decently and candidly, represented.' Hawkins knew Johnson in his early obscure years, and was acquainted with, though not always liked by, his friends. As an executor he had access to Johnson's personal papers. He was not afraid

to point out what he considered were Johnson's blemishes and weaknesses.

The book was also issued in connection with the first major collection of Johnson's *Works*, which came out in the same year. More comprehensive than any of its predecessors, Hawkins's *Life* was to hold its eminence until Boswell's overpowering invasion appeared.

Dr Johnson's House Trust

113 · 'THE LIFE OF SAMUEL JOHNSON, LLD'
James Boswell
Two volumes
London, Charles Dilly, 1791

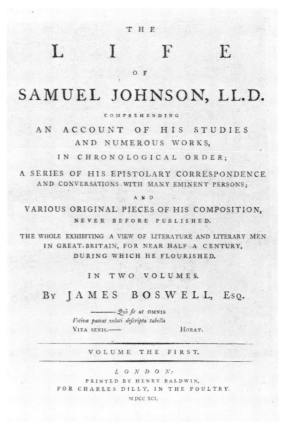

THE
LIFE
OF
SAMUEL JOHNSON, LL.D.
COMPREHENDING
AN ACCOUNT OF HIS STUDIES
AND NUMEROUS WORKS,
IN CHRONOLOGICAL ORDER;
A SERIES OF HIS EPISTOLARY CORRESPONDENCE
AND CONVERSATIONS WITH MANY EMINENT PERSONS;
AND
VARIOUS ORIGINAL PIECES OF HIS COMPOSITION,
NEVER BEFORE PUBLISHED.
THE WHOLE EXHIBITING A VIEW OF LITERATURE AND LITERARY MEN
IN GREAT-BRITAIN, FOR NEAR HALF A CENTURY,
DURING WHICH HE FLOURISHED.
IN TWO VOLUMES.
BY JAMES BOSWELL, ESQ.
— *Quò fit ut OMNIS*
Votiva pateat veluti descripta tabella
VITA SENIS.— HORAT.

VOLUME THE FIRST.

LONDON:
PRINTED BY HENRY BALDWIN,
FOR CHARLES DILLY, IN THE POULTRY.
M DCC XCI.

113

Inscribed:

   C. P. A. Dyce, and transcripts of Walpole's notes
Bookplate of: *Horace Walpole*
Vol. 1 showing title-page; Vol. 2 showing p. 583,
part of the summary of Johnson's character

Horace Walpole (1717–97), 4th Earl of Orford,
tolerated Boswell, but disliked Johnson intensely.
He was quick to read Boswell's biography, if only
to have the opportunity to damn it. Ten days after
the book came out he wrote to Mary Berry, on
26 May 1791:

> Boswell's book is gossiping, but have numbers of
> proper names, would be more readable, at least by
> me, were it reduced from two volumes to one –
> but there are woeful *longueurs*, both about his hero,
> and himself, the *fidus Achates*, about whom one has
> not the smallest curiosity.

In many ways, Walpole's views represent the super-
ficial assessment which is still prevalent. It is easy to
select the lively descriptions of Johnson's eccen-
tricities and his clever talk, and to ignore Boswell's
intention which is clearly stated in the sub-title. His
book was to deal with fifty years of exciting literary
history, with Johnson as the central figure. Although
Johnson was the recognized literary colossus, his
book was not to be his 'panegyrick', 'but his Life'. It
is also easy to imagine Boswell as the spy with his
notebook under the table, and to forget that he had

been an admirer of Johnson's works before they
met, and that his biography was the result of almost
twenty-five years of collecting material and careful
researches.

Victoria & Albert Museum, London (Dyce 1274)

114 · 'AN ESSAY ON THE LIFE AND GENIUS OF
SAMUEL JOHNSON, LLD'
Arthur Murphy
London, T. Longman and others, 1793
Showing pp. 84–5, a section of Murphy's
'paraphrastic translation' of Johnson's poem
'Know Thyself', written after finishing his revision
for the 4th edition of his *Dictionary*

In publicizing his own work Boswell did not hesitate
to point out the faults and inadequacies of Mrs Piozzi
and Hawkins as Johnson's biographers. Having used
Hawkins's book to prefix the first collected edition
of Johnson's works, the proprietors were now con-
templating another means, a shorter and less un-
wieldy assessment. Murphy's *Essay* duly came out,
independently as well as collectively with Johnson's
Works, first in 1792. As appropriate to his own
character, Murphy adopted a sagacious approach,
and gave a balanced and sometimes shrewd observation.

Dr Johnson's House Trust

SELECT BIBLIOGRAPHY

John F. Abbott, 'John Hawkesworth: Friend of Samuel Johnson and Editor of Captain Cook's *Voyages* and of *The Gentleman's Magazine*', *Eighteenth-Century Studies*, Vol. 3, Spring 1970, pp. 339–50

John F. Abbott, 'Dr Johnson and Dr Hawkesworth: A Literary Friendship', *The New Rambler*, Autumn 1971, pp. 2–17

Walter Jackson Bate, *Samuel Johnson*, London, 1978

Boswell's Life of Johnson, ed. G. B. Hill, revised and enlarged by E. F. Powell, 6 vols., Oxford, 1934–64: includes still the most comprehensive survey of the portraiture of Johnson, though Dr Powell's dating and attributions have not been followed entirely in this publication

O. M. Brack, Jr., and Robert B. Kelley (ed.), *The Early Biographies of Samuel Johnson*, Iowa City, 1974

A. M. Broadley, *Dr Johnson and Mrs Thrale*, London, 1910

James L. Clifford, *Young Samuel Johnson*, London, 1955

James L. Clifford, *Hester Lynch Piozzi (Mrs Thrale)*, 2nd edn, Oxford, 1968

James L. Clifford, *Dictionary Johnson*, London, 1980

R. W. Chapman and Allen T. Hazen, 'Johnson Bibliography: A Supplement to Courtney', *Proceedings of the Oxford Bibliographical Society*, V, 1939, pp. 119–66

J. A. Cochrane, *Dr Johnson's Printer: The Life of William Strahan*, Cambridge, Mass., 1964

William Prideaux Courtney and David Nichol Smith, *A Bibliography of Samuel Johnson*, illus. edn, Oxford, 1925

Sir Martin Davies, *National Gallery Catalogue. The British School*, London, 1946: the first to draw attention that the dating of Johnson's portraits by Reynolds is by no means straightforward

Bertram H. Davis, 'A Matter of Dispute: Thomas Percy and Samuel Johnson', *Transactions of the Johnson Society* (Lichfield), 1976, pp. 21–39

Bertram H. Davis, *A Proof of Eminence. The Life of Sir John Hawkins*, Bloomington and London, 1973

Bertram H. Davis, 'The Anonymous Letter Proposing Johnson's Pension', *Transactions of the Johnson Society* (Lichfield), 1981, pp. 35–9

Ada Earland, *John Opie and his Circle*, London, 1911

Charles N. Fifer, 'The Founding of Dr Johnson's Literary Club', *Notes & Queries*, July 1956, pp. 302–3

Charles N. Fifer, *The Correspondence of James Boswell with Certain Members of The Club*, London, 1976

J. D. Fleeman, *A Preliminary Handlist of Documents and Manuscripts of Samuel Johnson*, Oxford, 1967

J. D. Fleeman, 'The revenue of a writer. Samuel Johnson's literary earnings', *Studies in the Book Trade in Honour of Graham Pollard*, Oxford, 1975, pp. 211–30

J. D. Fleeman (introduction & notes), *The Sale Catalogue of Samuel Johnson's Library. A Facsimile Edition*, University of Victoria, 1975: reproduces no. 108 in facsimile

Lindsay Fleming, 'Dr Johnson's Use of Authorities in Compiling his Dictionary of English Language', *Notes & Queries*, June 1954, pp. 254–7, July pp. 294–7, August pp. 343–7

A. Graves and W. V. Cronin, *A History of the Works of Sir Joshua Reynolds*, 4 vols., privately printed, 1899–1901

Donald Greene, *Samuel Johnson's Library. An Annotated Guide*, University of Victoria, 1975

Isobel Grundy, 'A "Spurious" Poem by Lady Mary Wortley Montagu?', *Notes & Queries*, October 1980, pp. 407–10

Isobel Grundy, 'The Politics of Female Authorship. Lady Mary Wortley Montagu's reaction to the printing of her poems', *The Book Collector*, Spring 1982, pp. 19–37

Sir John Hawkins, *The Life of Samuel Johnson, LL.D.*, 2nd edn, London, 1787

Laetitia Matilda Hawkins, *Memoirs, Anecdotes, Facts and Opinions*, 2 vols., London, 1824

Abraham Hayward (ed.), *Autobiography, Letters and Literary Remains of Mrs Piozzi (Thrale)*, 2nd edn, 2 vols., London, 1861

Allen T. Hazen, *Samuel Johnson's Prefaces and Dedications*, New Haven, 1937

Frederick W. Hilles, *The Literary Career of Sir Joshua Reynolds*, Cambridge, 1936

Frederick W. Hilles (ed.), *Portraits by Sir Joshua Reynolds*, Melbourne, London, and Toronto, 1952

Frederick W. Hilles (ed.), *New Light on Dr Johnson*, New Haven, 1959

Derek Hudson, *Sir Joshua Reynolds. A Personal Study*, London, 1958

MARY HYDE, *The Impossible Friendship. Boswell and Mrs Thrale*, London, 1973

MARY HYDE, *The Thrales of Streatham Park*, Cambridge (Mass.), 1977

MARY HYDE, 'The Library Portraits at Streatham Park', *The New Rambler*, 1979, pp. 10–24

The Poems of Samuel Johnson, ed. David Nichol Smith and Edward L. McAdam, 2nd edn, Oxford, 1974

Samuel Johnson. The Complete English Poems, ed. J. D. Fleeman, Penguin Books, 1971

Johnson, Boswell, and Mrs Piozzi: A Suppressed Passage Restored, R. W. Chapman (ed.), London, 1929

The Queeney Letters, the Marquis of Lansdowne (ed.), London, 1934

The Letters of Samuel Johnson, R. W. Chapman (ed.), 3 vols., Oxford, 1952

The Works of Samuel Johnson, Sir John Hawkins (ed.), 11 vols., London, 1787

The Works of Samuel Johnson, 11 vols., Oxford, 1825

The Yale Edition of the Works of Samuel Johnson, New Haven and London, 1958–

Johnsonian Miscellanies, George Birbeck Hill (ed.), 2 vols., Oxford, 1897

HERMAN W. LIEBERT, 'Portraits of the Author: Lifetime Likenesses of Samuel Johnson', *English Portraits of the Seventeenth and Eighteenth Centuries*, Los Angeles, 1974, pp. 47–88

HERMAN W. LIEBERT, *Johnson's Head: The Story of the Bust of Dr Samuel Johnson Taken from the Life by Joseph Nollekens, R.A., in 1777* (Yale University Press 1960)

C. J. LONGMAN, *A Letter of Dr Johnson and some eighteenth century Imprints of the House of Longman*, privately printed, 1928

ROGER LONSDALE, *Dr Charles Burney. A Literary Biography*, Oxford, 1965

LAWRENCE C. MCHENRY, JR., and RONALD MACKEITH, 'Samuel Johnson's Childhood Illnesses and the King's Evil', *Medical History*, X, October 1966, pp. 386–99

LAWRENCE C. MCHENRY, JR., 'Samuel Johnson's Tics and Gesticulations', *Journal of the History of Medicine and Allied Sciences*, April 1967, Vol. XXII, no. 2

RONALD MACKEITH, 'The Death Mask of Samuel Johnson', *The New Rambler*, June 1968, pp. 41–7

A. EDWARD NEWTON, *This Book-Collecting Game*, Boston, 1928

JAMES NORTHCOTE, *The Life of Sir Joshua Reynolds*, 2nd edn, 2 vols., London, 1819

FREDERICK A. POTTLE, *The Literary Career of James Boswell*, Oxford, 1929

WILLIAM L. PRESSLY, *The Life and Art of James Barry*, New Haven and London, 1981

WILLIAM L. PRESSLY, *James Barry. The Artist as Hero*, London, 1983 (Tate Gallery exhibition catalogue)

SIR JAMES PRIOR, *Life of Edmond Malone*, London, 1860

Sir Joshua Reynolds. Discourses on Art, Robert R. Wark (ed.), New Haven and London, 1975

'The Ledgers of Sir Joshua Reynolds', Malcolm Cormack (ed.), *Walpole Society*, XLII, 1968–70, pp. 105–69

JOHN POPE ROGERS, *Opie and his Works*, London, 1878

J. CARTER ROWLAND, 'The Controversy over Johnson's Burial', *The New Rambler*, January 1970, pp. 5–10

J. H. SLEDD and G. J. KOLB, *Dr Johnson's Dictionary*, Chicago, 1955

DAVID NICHOL SMITH (ed.), *Eighteenth Century Essays on Shakespeare*, 2nd edn, Oxford, 1963

JAMES THOMAS SMITH, *A Book for a Rainy Day*, ed. Wilfred Whitten, London [1905]

JAMES THOMAS SMITH, *Nollekens and His Times*, ed. Wilfred Whitten, 2 vols., London, 1920

THOMAS TAYLOR, *A Life of John Taylor*, London [1911]

EUGENE THOMAS, 'Dr Johnson and his Amanuenses', *Transactions of the Johnson Society* (Lichfield), 1974, pp. 20–30

Thraliana. The Diary of Mrs Hester Lynch Thrale (Later Mrs Piozzi), ed. Katharine C. Balderston, 2nd edn, 2 vols., Oxford, 1951

ARTHUR TILLOTSON (ed.), *The Correspondence of Thomas Percy and Edmond Malone*, Louisiana State University Press, 1944

MARSHALL WAINGROW (ed.), *The Correspondence and other Papers of James Boswell Relating to the Making of the Life of Johnson*, New York and Toronto [1969]

JOHN WAIN, *Samuel Johnson*, New York, 1974

JOHN E. WALLIS, 'Dr Johnson and his English Dictionary', *Transactions of the Johnson Society* (Lichfield), 1945

Horace Walpole's Correspondence with Mary and Agnes Berry and Mary Cecilia Seton, ed. W. S. Lewis and A. Dayle Wallace, with assistance by Charles H. Bennett and Edwine M. Martz, London, 1944

SIR ELLIS K. WATERHOUSE, *Reynolds*, London, 1941

HENRY B. WHEATLEY, 'Johnson's Edition of Shakespeare', *The Athenaeum*, no. 4272, July–December 1909, p. 298

ROY MCKEEN WILES, 'The Contemporary Distribution of Johnson's *Rambler*', *Eighteenth-Century Studies*, Vol. 2, December 1968, pp. 155–71

K. K. YUNG, 'The Association Books of Johnson, Boswell, and Mrs Piozzi in the Johnson Birthplace Museum', *The New Rambler*, Spring 1972, pp. 23–44